Tourism in India

Potential, Problems and Prospects

Tourism in India

Potential, Problems and Prospects

Edited by

P.K. Mishra
Associate Professor and Head,
Department of Economic Studies,
Central University of Punjab, Bathinda

and

J.K. Verma
Assistant Professor,
Department of Economic Studies,
Central University of Punjab, Bathinda

New Century Publications
New Delhi, India

NEW CENTURY PUBLICATIONS
4800 / 24, Bharat Ram Road,
Ansari Road, Daryaganj,
New Delhi - 110 002 (India)

Tel.: 011-2324 7798, 4358 7398, 4101 7798
E-mail: indiatax@vsnl.com • info@newcenturypublications.com
www.newcenturypublications.com

Editorial office:
LG – 7, Aakarshan Bhawan,
4754-57/23, Ansari Road, Daryaganj,
New Delhi – 110 002

Tel.: 011-4356 0919

First Published: **2018**

ISBN: **978-81-7708-469-6**

Published by New Century Publications and printed at Milan Enterprises, New Delhi.

Designs: Patch Creative Unit, New Delhi.

PRINTED IN INDIA

About the Book

In the 21st Century, tourism has emerged as a leading sector across the globe. This sector has been widely acknowledged for its contribution to national income, foreign exchange reserves, employment creation, expansion of local business, poverty alleviation, infrastructure development, balanced regional development, cultural exchanges, and above all for developing and maintaining international relations and world peace. The development of tourism sector generates growth due to its linkage effects and cross-sectoral synergies which lead to the progress of other sectors including agriculture, handicrafts, healthcare, education, transport and communication, construction etc. On the social front, expansion of tourism brings positive changes in the population structure, occupational patterns, value system, individual behaviour, family relationships, collective lifestyles, moral conduct, creative expressions, traditional ceremonies and community organizations.

In India, tourism has become the most vibrant service sector activity and a multi-billion dollar industry over the years. The natural surroundings, architectural masterpieces, music, dance, paintings, customs and languages have all made India a tourist paradise. The strategies and policies of the Government of India including *Incredible India* and *Athithi Devo Bhava* have significantly contributed to the expansion of tourism in India.

The present volume contains 14 scholarly papers, authored by experts in the field, which not only provide an overview of the growth of tourism in India, but also give an analytical account of the problems and prospects associated with it.

About the Editors

Dr. P.K. Mishra is currently Associate Professor and Head of the Department of Economic Studies, Central University of Punjab, Bathinda. He has about 20 years of teaching and 10 years of research experience. He has to his credit 11 books and more than 110 research papers published in journals of national and international repute. His areas of specialization include development economics, tourism economics and social sector economics. He is a life member of Indian Econometric Society and Orissa Economic Association. He is associated with a number of prestigious national and international journals. He has delivered lectures and presented research papers at several national and international conferences.

Dr. J.K. Verma is presently Assistant Professor in the Department of Economic Studies, Central University of Punjab, Bathinda. He has about 5 years of teaching and research experience. He has to his credit about 20 research papers published in national and international journals of repute. His areas of specialization include development economics and entrepreneurship. He is life member of Indian Economic Association, Indian Commerce Association, and Indian Econometric Society. He is associated with a number of journals as editorial board member and reviewer. He has attended and presented papers at a number of national and international conferences/seminars.

Contents

Contributors

S.N. Tripathy	Professor of Economics (Retd.), Gokhale Institute of Politics and Economics, Pune, Maharashtra.
Chidanand Patil	Assistant Professor of Agri-Business, Central University of Punjab, Bathinda, Punjab.
Chaitra G.B.	Research Fellow of Agri-Business Management, University of Agricultural Sciences, Dharwad, Karnataka.
Parmjeet Kaur	Research Fellow of Economics, Central University of Punjab, Bathinda, Punjab.
Manpreet Kaur	Research Fellow of Economics, Central University of Punjab, Bathinda, Punjab.
V. Palanisingh	Research Fellow of Commerce, Alagappa University, Karaikudi, Tamil Nadu.
V. Abdul Salahudeen	Research Fellow of Commerce, Alagappa University, Karaikudi, Tamil Nadu.
T. R. Gurumoorthy	Professor of Commerce, Alagappa University, Karaikudi, Tamil Nadu.
Prashant H. Bhagat	Assistant Professor of Commerce, Chetana College, Bandra, Mumbai.
Naresh Singla	Assistant Professor of Economics, Central University of Punjab, Bathinda, Punjab.
Sarba N. Mishra	Associate Professor of Agricultural Economics, Orissa University of Agriculture and Technology, Bhubaneswar, Odisha.

Nirakar Pattanaik Research Fellow of Economics, Orissa University of Agriculture and Technology, Bhubaneswar, Odisha.

Aditya Kumar Tripathi Research Fellow of Management, Madan Mohan Malaviya University of Technology, Gorakhpur, Uttar Pradesh.

Rakesh Kumar Assistant Professor of Management, Madan Mohan Malaviya University of Technology, Gorakhpur, Uttar Pradesh.

Veenu Mehra Research Fellow of Education, Central University of Punjab, Bathinda, Punjab.

Biswajit Behera Assistant Professor of Education, Central University of Punjab, Bathinda, Punjab.

Naseer Ahmad Research Fellow of Environmental Sciences and Technology, Central University of Punjab, Bathinda, Punjab.

Puneeta Pandey Assistant Professor of Environmental Sciences and Management, Central University of Punjab, Bathinda, Punjab.

Harpreet Kaur Assistant Professor of Economics, Mata Sahib Kaur Girls College,Talwandi Sabo, Punjab.

Amandeep Kaur Research Fellow of Education, Central University of Punjab, Bathinda, Punjab.

Jubilee Padmanabhan Assistant Professor of Education, Central University of Punjab, Bathinda, Punjab.

Sandeep Research Fellow of Education, Central University of Punjab, Bathinda, Punjab.

Shamshir Singh Dhillon Assistant Professor of Education, Central University of Punjab, Bathinda, Punjab.

Introduction by the Editors

Right since ancient times, travel and tourism have been at the centre stage of socio-economic, cultural and political development of a nation. It has been portrayed as a panacea for many evils such as underdevelopment, unemployment, poverty, regional imbalances, social discrimination and environmental degradation. Its huge potential in contributing to income generation, job creation, infrastructure development, foreign exchange earnings, export promotion, and poverty reduction has been well recognized across the globe.

In India, tourism has been identified as one of the drivers for promoting faster, sustainable and more inclusive economic growth. India's travel and tourism industry ranked seventh in terms of its total contribution to the country's gross domestic product and second in terms of total employment support in the world in 2016. The sector is predicted to contribute to 10 percent of gross domestic product and 9.6 percent of total employment by 2027. Indian tourism, though, historically famous for pilgrimage and heritage tourism, has recently been marching ahead with eco-tourism, medical tourism, adventure tourism, rural tourism, cruise tourism, argi-tourism, and MICE tourism. The presence of socio-cultural diversity, large variety of flora and fauna, majestic forts, religious monuments, and urban and rural sites has been catalysts in the rapid growth of tourism in India. Complementary to this, the appropriate government strategies and polices are also adding to the strengths of tourism in India.

Tourism is an important social phenomenon in almost every society due to the basic human tendency of acquiring new and memorable experiences concerning adventurous activities, learning, and amusement. The basic human urge to know about unreached parts of the globe/region has been an important driving force that is fostering tourism. It has been aptly remarked 'travelling unveils new dimensions of this world not known to the naked eye'. In recent decades, improvements in knowledge domain, advances in technology, reduction in communication barriers, progress in transportation and development of tourist-friendly facilities, have all contributed to the significant growth of tourism.

It has been rightly said that 'tourism is having the ability to generate socio-economic opportunities, and help reducing the gap between the rich and the poor which is more important than ever'. Tourism has been widely acknowledged for its contribution to national income, foreign exchange reserves, employment creation, expansion of local business, poverty alleviation, infrastructure development, improving balanced regional development, augmenting cultural exchanges, and maintaining international relations and world peace. Tourism is complementary and supplementary to the progress of other sectors including agriculture, handicrafts, healthcare, education, transport and communication, construction etc. On the social front, expansion of tourism brings about positive changes in the population structure, occupational patterns, value system, individual behaviour, family relationships, collective lifestyles, moral conduct, creative expressions, traditional ceremonies and community organizations. From the environment point of view, tourism is critical in reducing environmental degradation and making available a clean environment for the use of future generations. In toto, the sector is pivotal in bringing about a more equitable distribution of national income and wealth thereby making the growth process more inclusive and sustainable.

Tourism in India has got its existence since a long time when it was recognised as travel by people in search of knowledge and peace. The Vedic period termed tourism in the form of pilgrimage or *dham yatra*. The *Arthashastra* of Kautilya also recognised tourism in the form of travel across the country. India has always been a country of spiritual integrity and nationalism with unity in diversity. The diversity is seen in people of India in terms of language and culture, food and festivals, dresses and costumes, caste and religions, flora and fauna, and also in varying landscapes. India's rich cultural heritage, historically significant places, long coastal belts, and hillocks are so beautiful and serene that all these attract the tourists from each and every corner of the world.

The bounteous heritage, beautiful architecture, glorious traditions, rich and diverse cultures, languages, magnificent music, dance and paintings, mesmerizing and scenic landscapes, snow-clad peaks of the Himalayas, alluring beaches, and the ornate temples have all made India a tourist paradise. India has succeeded in becoming the most preferred destination amongst domestic and overseas travellers. Tourism in India has been instrumental in generating foreign exchange, creating employment opportunities, and generating household income over the years. It has brought the opportunity of infrastructure development and has helped in regional and economic development. Moreover, it has been a significant growth driver and a means of poverty alleviation.

In spite of such growth performances, tourism in India faces a number of problems which retards its full potential. The principle issues and challenges include poor transportation facilities to places of natural beauty and places having the potential of being a part of eco-tourism, lack of availability of basic hygienic amenities at halting points for tourists, lack of adequate tourism and hospitality infrastructure, poor maintenance of small but significant heritages, lack of safety and security at many tourism sites, lack of adequate information about many tourism sites, and lack of proper promotional strategies for innovative tourism products. The timely address of these problems calls for due attention of both public and private stakeholders of travel and tourism in India.

It is in this backdrop that this volume compiles 14 scholarly writings of experts in the field which evaluate the present state of tourism in India and identify opportunities for its promotion and expansion, and suggest ways out for the possible threats in its growth path.

S.N. Tripathy in his paper *Growth of Tourism in India: Problems and Prospects* attempts to present the trend and growth of tourism sector thereby suggesting policy paradigms imperative for the promotion of tourism as a means of accelerating the socio-economic development of the nation.

Chidanand Patil and Chaitra G.B. in their paper *Growth and Performance of Indian Tourism Industry* evaluate the growth performance of tourism in India and its contribution to income and employment generation at the macro level.

Parmjeet Kaur and Manpreet Kaur in their paper *Services Trade of India and Tourism* examine the growth trends of India's tourism trade with the rest of the world and also assesses the revealed comparative advantage of India's tourism sector.

V. Palanisingh, V. Abdul Salahudeen and T.R. Gurumoorthy in their paper *Tourism Industry in India: Gears and Glows* attempt to examine correlations between exchange rate and foreign tourist arrivals, between exchange rate and foreign exchange earnings, and also between government spending, capital investment and foreign tourist arrivals. The paper on the basis of the presence of high degrees of correlations, suggests focusing on exchange rate stability and foreign tourist arrivals in India.

Prashant H. Bhagat in his paper *Incredible India Campaign: Opportunities and Challenges for Tourism* tries to identify the opportunities and challenges associated with the Incredible India campaign, and makes suggestions for making this campaign an effective means of promoting tourism in the country.

Manpreet Kaur and Naresh Singla in their paper *Global Emergence of Agri-tourism: Implications for India* attempt to assess the worldwide spread of agri-tourism, particularly by reviewing country-specific case studies globally, thereby drawing ways and adequate policy options to develop agrarian economy in the light of agri-tourism in India.

Sarba N. Mishra and Nirakar Pattanaik in their paper *Medical Tourism in India: An Emerging Market* evaluate the emerging medical tourism sector in India, and make suggestions for the improvement of medical tourism in the country.

Aditya Kumar Tripathi and Rakesh Kumar in their paper *Role of Social Media in the Promotion of Tourism* reflect on the role that social media play sin promoting tourism in India. Particularly, it focuses on the roles played by Facebook, Twitter, YouTube, Instagram and Linkedin.

Veenu Mehra in her paper *Electronic Tourism (E-tourism) and Sustainable Development* highlights the vision of e-tourism and also points out the challenges of e-tourism in the sustainable growth of tourism in India.

Biswajit Behera in his paper *Sustainable Tourism: A Pedagogical Approach* attempts to develop an approach towards sustainability in tourism education, and recommends a guiding prototype for sustainable tourism pedagogy to set a direction for further research and practical implementation.

Naseer Ahmad and Puneeta Pandey in their paper *Tourism in Jammu and Kashmir: Economic and Environmental Consequences* emphasize on the economic contributions of tourism in Jammu and Kashmir while focusing on its environmental consequences.

Harpreet Kaur in her paper *Promotion of Tourism in Punjab: Problems and Prospects* highlights the current status, problems and prospects of tourism promotion in Punjab.

Amandeep Kaur and Jubliee Padmanabhan in their paper *Social Responsibility, Tourism and Sustainable Development* highlight the perspectives of social responsibility in tourism and argue that the codes of good practices in tourism needs to be respected and implemented by all the stakeholders of tourism.

Sandeep and Shamshir Singh Dhillon in their paper *Social Value Creation through Development of Tourism* highlight both positive and negative impacts of tourism on social values and point out the means of maximizing the positive impacts and eliminating the negative impacts.

Acknowledgements

We take this opportunity to express our deep appreciation

and gratitude to the authors of the papers for their scholarly contributions to this volume. Their research findings and observations will surely add to the existing body of literature on the subject of tourism. This work, we hope, will certainly be instrumental for all those interested in understanding the contemporary trends, patterns, issues and challenges of tourism in India.

We sincerely express our gratefulness to our patron Professor R.K. Kohli, Honourable Vice-Chancellor, Central University of Punjab, Bathinda who has been a source of unceasing inspiration and unparalleled encouragement in our entire academic and research initiatives.

We extend deepest gratitude to Professor P. Ramarao, Dean, Academic Affairs, Central University of Punjab, Bathinda who has constantly tendered valuable advices on all key matters concerning academics and research.

We also express our heartfelt thankfulness to all our colleagues who have been constant sources of motivation, encouragement and support for bringing this volume to the limelight.

We sincerely acknowledge the support received from the Ministry of Tourism, Government of India.

Finally, we express our thanks to Mr. Sandeep Sury, Chief Executive, New Century Publications, New Delhi and his team of editors for their meticulous and untiring co-operation and endeavour for timely publication of this volume.

Bathinda

P.K. Mishra
J.K. Verma

1

Growth of Tourism in India: Problems and Prospects

S.N. Tripathy

Introduction

According to the World Tourism Organization (WTO), tourism is defined by "the set of activities of a person travelling to a place outside his or her usual environment for at least one night, but less than a year, and whose main purpose of travel is other than experience of an activity remunerated from the place visited". *Tourism industry* means and includes all tourism products, infrastructure, facilities and services that attract tourists and make their visit and stay as comfortable and meaningful as possible. *Tourists* mean all people travelling into the state for the purpose of undertaking leisure, business, education, medical treatment and other relevant activities but without the objective of setting up domicile. As tourism has assumed a new dimension, it becomes essential to make an in-depth study of various aspects related to it. Travel and tourism has acquired importance over a period of time next to oil industry. Realizing the importance of tourism, Government of India has started taking necessary steps to develop this vast potential area.

Tourism has been recognized as a smokeless industry pertaining to people, transporting them to a designated destination, putting them comfortably as their pockets permit, entertaining them and sending them back with sweet memories. Tourism has been growing fast in encompassing manner with visible socio-economic manifestations. Its transformation process has also been equally fascinating with new consumer groups of distinct travel.

In this backdrop, this paper briefly outlines the growth of tourism sector and its contribution in India, highlights the problems connected with the tourism industry, and finally makes suggestions for the development of tourism in the country. Keeping these objectives in view, the present study has been undertaken with the help of secondary sources of data collected from the published sources mainly books, Government reports and papers, internet etc. The publications and data available from the Ministry of Tourism, Government of India have been extensively used for documenting this paper.

Tourism and its Dimensions

In 1988, the World Tourism Organization (WTO) defined sustainable tourism as 'leading to management of all resources in such a way that economic, social and aesthetic needs can be fulfilled while maintaining cultural integrity, essential ecological processes, biological diversity and life support systems'. Later in 1992, the 'Earth Summit' in Rio established the triple principles of environmental, economic and social sustainability. Since then, the principles of sustainable tourism have been adopted by the tourism industry worldwide.

An important aspect of the tourism industry, which is of specific significance to India, is its contribution to national integration and preservation of natural as well as cultural environments and enrichment of the social and cultural lives of the people. India provides enormous experiential opportunities for tourists based on a wide variety of all-season attractions available throughout the country.

It is imperative that these attractions get developed for the socio-economic benefit of the local communities, especially in order to strengthen inclusive economic growth. It is equally important to ensure that increased socio-economic well-being does not cause permanent or long-term damage to the country's physical, cultural and environmental heritage. The use of existing resources, both tangible and intangible, has to be undertaken judiciously for the well-being of the present generation but not at the cost of depriving future generations of any part of our inheritance. The Planning Commission in the Approach Paper to the Twelfth Five Year Plan (2012-17) has mentioned that tourism and hospitality sector has a key role to play in promoting faster, sustainable and more inclusive economic growth. The importance of sustainable tourism worldwide has increased significantly due to the impact of increased human activity on climate. It is necessary that the negative impact of the tourism industry is not enlarged unrealistically. Full advantage can then be drawn from the potential of tourism for inclusive growth with livelihoods support to the poor, most disadvantaged, women and youth.

For conceptualizing a system of Sustainable Tourism Criteria for India (STCI), Ministry of Tourism appoints a lead consultant, who may work with a consortium, to provide a detailed operational plan for the implementation of STCI. The actual inspection and audit of applicants to the STCI system is usually entrusted to an independent professionally acknowledged third party.

The funding for the implementation of the STCI system is met from ongoing schemes—market research, professional services, capacity building for service providers, and domestic promotion and publicity. A project monitoring unit (PMU) is created in the Ministry with the specific purpose of administering the STCI system. Tourism development must be sustainable environmentally, socially, economically and culturally. Sustainable tourism must ensure quality of life of the people, good experience for the tourists and maintain quality of environment alive to the requirements to protect the haphazard growth in sensitive areas. Government has enacted a number of legislations such as the Forest Conservation Act, 1980, Wild Life (Protection Act), 1972, Environment Protection Act, 1986 and Coastal Regulatory Zone Act, 1991 in this regard.

Eco-tourism

Eco-tourism is a form of sustainable tourism. Eco-tourism refers to tourism activities in ecologically sensitive areas in a manner that conserves the environment and improves the well-being of the local people. The development of eco-tourism in many areas of the world clearly indicates that this form of tourism has great potential in India because of the richness of its flora and fauna and the wide range of ecosystems including mountains, coasts, rivers, forests, deserts and grasslands. Whilst the negative impacts of tourism are well-known, there are also great examples of eco-tourism good practices. Implementation and participation in eco-tourism activities includes adherence to the following principles:

1. Minimize impact on environment.
2. Build environmental and cultural awareness and respect.
3. Provide positive experiences for both visitors and host communities.
4. Provide financial benefits for conservation as well as to local communities.
5. Implement leanings from best practices.

Based on eco-system network model, a sustainable planning and marketing orientation does not just satisfy the needs and wants of an individual but it strives to attain a sustained ecosystem. The benefits are not just profits but civic energy and social unity. Competition is replaced by dynamic interaction that aims at environmental, social and economic equity within the local-global network of living and physical structures.

Heritage Tourism

Travellers have been going round the world since ages to experience the culture and heritage of different societies, but in the modern era such travels have increased exponentially. With UNESCO having started the process of declaring historically important sites as 'World Heritage Sites', heritage tourism has acquired global dimensions. In India, which has a rich heritage, a significant share of all domestic and foreign tourism activities have centred on its heritage sites.

While tangible heritage has been in the mainstream of tourism development in India, the intangible and living heritage has not attracted much attention. There is a need to analyse this segment to see how best these assets can be utilized to provide new cultural experiences to tourists. Development of tourism activities relating to intangible heritage has to be carried out in a sensitive manner so as to ensure that socio-economic benefits accrue to the communities but at the same time the values or practices constituting the essence of intangible heritage do not get irreparably dented by over-commercialization or insensitive development.

Intangible heritage, which includes folklore, cuisine, customary practices, etc., needs to be identified in all States and Union Territories of the country. While some of this information may already be available with different sources, it would have to be collated and compiled, and supplemented with primary surveys/studies. There is also a need for mapping the requirements in order to make these heritage characteristics attractive for tourists. In addition, our rich spiritual heritage attracts many international tourists as well. Our spiritual heritage also therefore needs to be mapped and user needs identified for planned development.

Village and Rural Tourism

India's 5,000 years of history, its length, breadth and the variety of geographical features make its tourism basket large and varied. It presents heritage and cultural along with medical, business and sports tourism. Tourism in India is one of the largest service industries, with a contribution of about 6 percent to the national GDP and 9.24 percent of the total employment in India.

Rural tourism needs to be given an impetus by earmarking funds for pilot projects on the basis of a model plan for each State for the purpose. These villages can be taken up for priority development particularly if the projects can be linked with the restoration of heritage properties in the area. This would provide a boost to local performing arts and help conserve the local culture apart from preventing rural-urban migration. Local people in the rural areas should be encouraged to participate in tourism related projects, which may preferably be formulated by the tourist officials in consultation with locals and NGOs. These projects could be in the nature of providing glimpse of the village ambience and the tourists can be presented with local cuisine, art and culture by persons in local costumes engaging in the daily activities of cooking, weaving, dancing etc. Moderate, but clean, accommodations for tourists should be constructed by villagers in traditional design and architecture. Bank finances should be made available at attractive terms and conditions for promotion of such projects.

The diversity of wild life in India is as rich as that of its flora and fauna. The great wealth of Indian wild life can be imagined with the sight of majestic elephants, the dance of peacocks, the camel strides, the roar of tigers with unparalleled acts of beauty. Watching birds and animals in their natural habitat is an experience in itself. The vastness of wild life and wilderness is India is unparalleled in the world. All these account for the immense opportunities for wild life tourism in India. The immense heritage of wild life in India comprises of 80 national parks and another whopping 441 wild life sanctuaries including the bird sanctuaries.

These reserves and forest areas are spread across the breadth and length right from the foot hills of Himalayan Jim Corbett National park to six national parks in Andaman, from Ranthambore National Park in Rajasthan to Hazaribag Wild Life Sanctuary in Bihar. India also boasts of the unique ecosystem at Sunderbans which is a UNESCO world heritage site and home to the largest number of tigers in the world.

The success of future tourism is intrinsically connected with the way in which the industry and the tourism system understand and incorporate the emerging critical trends that support its expansion. Tourism is undergoing major changes: aging world population (Western countries) and active lifestyle of older travellers, the emerging markets, growing disposable income of the youth and awareness about impact of tourism on environment, will decisively influence the number of tourists, motivation, destination and product choices as well as activities of the future travellers. The rapid liberalization and deregulation of markets will bring fierce competition based on price, quality and characteristics of the tourism products. These trends will bring profound changes in the management and planning of tourism business and destination.

While global trends push forward new managerial approaches, the managers and planners must be aware of the emerging tools that help to manage and market business and destinations. Future trends point towards three strategic directions: satisfying consumers, destination development and management and territory organisations. Destinations face increasing challenges in international market place where numerous stakeholders (tourists, local people, tour operators, hotels and restaurants owners etc.) with diverse values and often divergent needs compete for scarce resources. The growing population of travellers and inhabitants increasingly make impact on natural and social environment.

The integrated destination management brings in destinations ecological-human communities as equitable and integrated members of planning and marketing and goal setting. The new approach integrates economic mobility, social equity and environmental responsibilities towards achieving the equality of life within the living system.

India provides enormous experiential opportunities for tourists based on a wide variety of all-season attractions available throughout the country. It is imperative that these attractions get developed for the socio-economic benefit of the local communities, especially in order to strengthen inclusive economic growth. It is equally important to ensure that increased socio-economic well-being does not cause permanent or long-term damage to the country's physical, cultural and environmental heritage. The use of existing resources, both tangible and intangible, has to be undertaken judiciously for the well-being of the present generation but not at the cost of depriving future generations of any part of our inheritance.

The Planning Commission in the Approach Paper to the Twelfth Five Year Plan (2012-17) has mentioned that tourism and hospitality sector has a key role to play in promoting faster, sustainable and more inclusive economic growth. The importance of sustainable tourism worldwide has increased significantly due to the impact of increased human activity on climate. It is necessary that the negative impact of the tourism industry is not enlarged unrealistically. Full advantage can then be drawn from the potential of tourism for inclusive growth with livelihoods support to the poor, most disadvantaged, women and youth.

1. The criteria and indicators of sustainable tourism for tour operators and the accommodation sector, especially rural tourism, should be finalized for implementation.
2. For conceptualizing a system of Sustainable Tourism Criteria for India (STCI), Ministry of Tourism should appoint a lead consultant, who may work with a consortium, to provide a detailed operational plan for the implementation of STCI.
3. The actual inspection and audit of applicants to the STCI system may be entrusted to an independent professionally acknowledged third party.
4. The funding for the implementation of the STCI system should be met from the ongoing schemes for market research, professional services, capacity building for service providers, and domestic promotion and publicity.
5. A project monitoring unit (PMU) is created in the Ministry with the specific purpose of administering the STCI system.
6. Financial assistance under the Ministry's Market

Development Assistance scheme should be provided for representatives of recognized national associations to participate in workshops/seminars on sustainable tourism organized by reputed organizations in India and abroad.

Intangible heritage, which includes folklore, cuisine, customary practices, etc., needs to be identified in all States and Union Territories of the country. While some of this information may already be available with different sources, it would should be collated and compiled, and supplemented with primary surveys/studies. There is also a need for mapping the requirements in order to make these heritage characteristics attractive for tourists. In addition, our rich spiritual heritage attracts many international tourists as well. Our spiritual heritage also therefore needs to be mapped and user needs identified for planned development. In the Twelfth Five Year Plan (2012-17), the Ministry of Tourism provided funds to States/UTs for undertaking studies, through competent professional agencies, for identification and mapping of the intangible heritage, including spiritual heritage. A study in each State should also be undertaken to list all heritage sites and heritage buildings in association with State or national level organisations.

The success of tourism depends on the ability of the firms to engage in sustainable use and conservation of vital resources. Destination development is the key to sustaining the natural and cultural resources on which tourism depends. Therefore, steps have been taken up as key initiatives for the development of tourism destinations. The close interaction between the public sector, the destination tourism marketing organisations, private sector and local residents in planning is the key principle for sustainable tourism. Thus, the stakeholders can work most effectively together to manage local and global influences on their natural and cultural resources. Effective destination development is the important problem facing the tourism managers today.

Contribution of Tourism to Indian Economy

Tourism has the potential to stimulate other economic factors through its forward and backward linkages with a host of related sectors like agriculture, manufacturing, transport, hospitality, education, health, banking, etc. Expenditure on tourism induces a chain of transactions requiring supply of goods and services from these associated sectors. The economic benefits that flow into the economy through growth of tourism in the form of increased national and state revenues, business receipts, employment, wages and salary income, buoyancy in Central, State and local tax receipts can contribute towards overall socio-economic improvement and accelerate the growth of the economy. India needs to reap the full potential of a vibrant tourism sector.

In fact, India has witnessed enormous progress in the tourism sector regards its rank in the Travel and Tourism Competitiveness Index (TTCI). Rank of India in TTCI Report of 2017 was 40 as compared to 52 in 2015, 65 in 2013 and 68 in 2011. India's travel and tourism sector ranks 7th in the world in terms of its total contribution to the country's GDP, according to a report of the World Travel and Tourism Council (WTTC). The tourists have a better appreciation of the cultural diversity of India. Tourism also encourages preservation of monuments and heritage properties and helps in the survival of arts forms, crafts and culture.

Table 1.1 reveals that with regard to the number of domestic tourist visits in 2016, Tamil Nadu's share was 21.3 percent followed by Uttar Pradesh at 13.1 percent whereas Andhra Pradesh occupies the third position with a 9.5 percent of the total share during the same year.

In 2016, the tourism industry facilitated in generating 25,400,000 jobs which constituted about 5.8 percent of the total employment. Tourism sector has tremendous potential to increase if budgetary allocations are hiked from 0.9 percent of the total allocation to 1.5 percent in 2018-19. The aggregate contribution of travel and tourism to Indian GDP was US$ 208.9 billion which constitutes 9.6 percent of the GDP in 2016 with a prospect to increase by 6.7 percent in 2017 and 10 percent of the GDP by 2027 (www.assocham.org).

Table 1.1: Percentage Share of Top 10 States of India in Terms of Domestic Tourist Visits in 2016

Rank	State/UT	Percent Share
1.	Tamil Nadu	21.3
2.	Uttar Pradesh	13.1
3.	Andhra Pradesh	9.5
4.	Madhya Pradesh	9.3
5.	Karnataka	8.0
6.	Maharashtra	7.2
7.	Telangana	5.9
8.	West Bengal	4.6
9.	Gujarat	2.6
10.	Rajasthan	2.6
	Total of top 10 states	84.2
	Others	15.8
	Total	100.0

Source: State/UT Tourism Development.

Tourism sector has immense backward and forward linkages in terms of both income and employment and can contribute significantly to the economy. A resourceful and innovative approach keeping in view the socio-demographic changes taking place world-wide and an efficient information system would yield better results. At the same time, the need for sound perspective planning with local participation is imperative.

The total contribution of travel and tourism to Indian GDP was US$ 208.9 billion, i.e. 9.6 percent of GDP in 2016, and is projected to rise to 6.7 percent in 2017 and 10 percent of the GDP in 2027. Further, travel and tourism investment in 2016 accounted for 5.7 percent of the total investment (US$ 34 billion). It should rise by 4.5 percent in 2017 and 5.7 percent per annum over the next ten years to US$ 61.8 billion in 2027. According to the data, the travel and tourism sector generated ₹ 14.1 trillion (US$ 208.9 billion) in 2016, which is world's

7th largest in terms of absolute size; the sum is equivalent to 9.6 percent of India's GDP. Additionally, the sector created 40.3 million jobs in 2016, which ranks India 2nd in the world in terms of total employment generated. The sector accounts for 9.3 percent of the country's total jobs.

It also noted that India witnessed 8 million foreign tourist arrivals in calendar year 2015. As per Economist Intelligence Unit (EIU) [1] estimates, the number of foreign tourist arrivals is expected to rise up to 12 million by 2019, growing at a CAGR [2] of 9.2 percent.

With the inclusion of non-resident Indians among international tourists, India has skipped from 16th place in the revised World Tourism Organisation (WTO) [3] rankings to settle at 24th for 2014 and 2015. The rank of India in international tourist arrivals in both 2014 and 2015 in the latest UNWTO's World Tourism Barometer, as of March 2017, is 24th as against the previous ranks of 41st and 40th in 2014 and 2015, respectively, as per a press release issued by the Ministry of Tourism.

A study jointly conducted by ASSOCHAM and Yes Bank has proposed developmental interventions including tourism infrastructure development and the emergence of tourism themes. The National Tourism Authority (NTA) can act as a nodal agency for undertaking a wide range of activities like investment promotion, marketing, escalation resolutions, development planning and implementation, coordination etc.

The travel and tourism industry has tremendous potential to rise by 2.5 percent provided the budgetary allocation is enhanced from the current 0.9 percent of the total allocation to at least 1.5 percent in 2018-19. It has proposed developmental interventions including tourism infrastructure development and the emergence of tourism themes.

The total contribution of travel and tourism to Indian GDP was US$ 208.9 billion i.e. 9.6 percent of GDP in 2016, and is expected to rise by 6.7 percent in 2017 and 10.0 percent of GDP in 2027. Further, travel and tourism investment in 2016 accounted for 5.7 percent of the total investment (US$ 34 billion). It should rise by 4.5 percent in 2017 and 5.7 percent per annum over the next ten years to US$ 61.8 billion in 2027.

Foreign Tourist Arrivals in India

The Indian slogan *athithi devo bhava* means that guests are like God and our courteous attitude reflects our inner self. Indians have been highly hospitable and this trend is still present in modern India. Intricate arrangements are made for a guest who comes home for a holiday. Foreigners love India as it is a storehouse of art, culture, dance and drama. The ethnic culture is present in clothing which attracts several shoppers who love to collect trinkets and serious artefacts. Responsible tourism is conducted by way of giving the tourist the right concept in tours.

Their accommodation in government lodges and private hotels is always a luxury. The importance to tourism is essential as they carry the picture of our culture and hospitality. In the economic context, foreign currency in India can be gathered via tourism. Several tourist spots do well all throughout the year and special seasons do exceptionally well as the foreigners throng the place for sight-seeing trips. A trip for any visitor has to be trouble free. Taxi cabs, translation books and a dependable guide make the trip interesting. The hygiene conditions in the tourist areas are improving and well maintained hotels and tourist sports are an all-around attraction.

The Ministry of Tourism is looking for new ways to encourage tourism in India. It is very much essential for a visitor to enjoy the stay and this is enhanced by facilities like road transport, guides and good hotels. Many hotels have multi-cuisine to accommodate the choices of foreigners who generally find the Indian food very spicy. Tour operators are very systematic with their plans. Complete details about weather conditions, clothes required and facilities are given to the tourists to help them prepare for a holiday.

In fact, foreign tourists from all over the world spend more in India than almost any other country worldwide, according to Economy Watch. Tourists are attracted by India's cultural diversity, temples, scenery and festivals. Each region of India offers something for foreign visitors, from the Taj Mahal and New Delhi in the north, to bustling Mumbai in the West to the religious centres of Varanasi in central India and number of beaches in the coastal cities.

So far, as the number of foreign tourist visits in 2016 is concerned, Table 1.2 reveals that Tamil Nadu's share was 19.1 percent followed by Maharashtra at 18.9 percent whereas Uttar Pradesh occupies the third position with 12.8 percent of the total share during the year 2016.

Table 1.2: Percentage Share of Top 10 States in Foreign Tourists Visits in 2016

Rank	State/UT	Percent share
1.	Tamil Nadu	19.1
2.	Maharashtra*	18.9
3.	Uttar Pradesh	12.8
4.	Delhi**	10.2
5.	West Bengal	6.2
6.	Rajasthan	6.1
7.	Kerala	4.2
8.	Bihar	4.1
9.	Goa	2.8
10.	Punjab	2.7
	Total of top 10 states	87.0
	Others	13.0
	Total	100.0

Source: State/UT Tourism Development.

*Estimated using all-India growth rate.

**Estimated using growth rate of foreign tourists' arrival at Delhi airport.

According to 'India Tourism Statistics at a Glance, 2017', released by the Union Ministry of Tourism along with the Bureau of Immigration, India recorded 14.57 million international tourist arrivals in 2016, a 9.6 percent increase over 2015. During the first six months of 2017, India welcomed 4.89 million foreign tourist arrivals recording a 17.2 percent growth over the same time period in 2016. WTTC opined that India's figures are predominantly generated by domestic travel, which accounts for 88 percent of the sector's contribution to GDP in 2016. Money spent by foreign travellers in India, only represents 12 percent of tourism revenues and in 2016 it totalled ₹ 1.5 trillion (US$ 22.8 billion). Data from the UN World Tourism Organisation (UNWTO) shows that India received only 9 million international arrivals in 2016, placing it at 40th place in the world; a tenth of those received by top-ranking France.

However, currently India has started compiling the data arrivals of non-resident Indians (NRIs) also. "Due to this inclusion, India's improved rank reflecting the true and comparable scenario has now been acknowledged by the UNWTO", the release said. With this inclusion, the share of India in the ITAs has also increased from 0.68 percent (based on FTAs) to 1.12 percent in 2015.

Table 1.3 depicts the top 10 source countries for foreign tourist arrivals (FTAs) in India in 2016.

Future Prospects of Tourism

India is a favoured tourism destination in the tourism markets overseas. To promote various Indian tourism products vis-à-vis competition faced from various other destinations and to increase India's share of the global tourism market, an integrated marketing and promotional strategy comprising centralized media campaigns launched by the Ministry and a wide range of promotional activities undertaken by the 14 India tourism offices overseas has been undertaken.

Under this scheme, the Ministry has launched a multi-pronged promotional campaign in key markets across the world under the banner of 'Incredible India'. The Incredible India campaigns aim to position the country as a destination for discerning travellers, focusing on the diversity of India as a holiday destination with 'something for everyone'. It includes a wide ranging advertising campaign in prime print publications, a global television campaign encompassing prominent channels and an innovative online campaign on the world's most popular websites. This convergence of media for promotion has brought great visibility and built awareness for the 'Incredible India' brand.

Table 1.3: Top 10 Source Countries for Foreign Tourist Arrivals (FTAs) in India in 2016

S. No.	Source Country	Percent Share
1.	Bangladesh	15.68
2.	United States	14.73
3.	United Kingdom	10.70
4.	Canada	3.60
5.	Malaysia	3.43
6.	Sri Lanka	3.38
7.	Australia	3.33
8.	Germany	3.02
9.	China	2.85
10.	France	2.71
	Total top 10 countries	63.44
	Others	36.56
	Grand total	100.0

Source: Bureau of Immigration, Government of India.

The country has vast and varied potential, which is still waiting for proper use, meaning it is a scarce sensitive recourse of the sub-continent. Thus, it was indeed a trade phenomenon in the past, but now it has grown into a "trade" by itself—rather the most productive industry inducing many activities. The spatial aspects like locations, spatial interactions within close and open systems are inherent features of tourism. Tourism in the country has the potential to emerge as a key economic driver. It is estimated that tourism can generate employment next only to the construction sector.

As the backbone of any economy, the provision of infrastructure is a prerequisite towards attaining economic growth and also improving the country's tourism capacity. To add upon, the anticipated growth of the Indian economy is expected to exert more pressure on infrastructure support facilities. The infrastructural bottlenecks need to be unleashed to enhance the visitor's experience manifold. There are two major objectives for developing the tourism infrastructure sector: (a) to provide adequate, convenient, fast and safe facilities which are competitively priced services to meet the primary needs of the domestic and foreign tourists, and (b) to provide the multi-dimensional requirement of Indian tourism industry with support facilities and act as a catalyst to economic development of the country.

In India, the tourism sector is based on exploiting its unique endowments of biodiversity, forests, rivers, and its rich culture and heritage. The challenges in this sector lie in successfully preserving these in their original form, and making them accessible to domestic and international travellers. Tourism in India has the potential to create economic interest of local communities in the protection of its natural and cultural endowments leading to a more sustainable growth.

According to the latest Tourism Satellite Accounting (TSA) research, released by the World Travel and Tourism Council (WTTC) and its strategic partner Oxford Economics, the demand for travel and tourism in India is expected to grow by 8.2 percent between 2016 and 2019 and will place India at the third position in the world. India's travel and tourism sector is expected to be the second largest employer in the world, employing 40,037,000 by 2019. Capital investment in India's travel and tourism sector is expected to grow at 8.8 percent between 2016 and 2019. The report forecasts India to get capital investment worth US$ 94.5 billion in the travel and tourism sector in 2019. India is projected to become the fifth fastest growing business travel destination from 2016-2019 with an estimated real growth rate of 7.6 percent.

Despite its high potential, the current scenario in the Indian tourism industry has problems like:

1. Inadequate accommodation capacity.
2. Lack of supportive infrastructure—roads, health and hygiene, communication gaps, etc.
3. Costly travel—gap between demand and supply of infrastructure.
4. Lapses in security and safety.

Therefore, sustainable tourism marketing objectives are not to design product, price, place of a tourism destination or attraction, but to ensure quality of life and environment through tourism development. Achieving this will be a challenge. It involves developing an interactive product or place relationship that will give value to visitors and to diverse community stakeholders.

Although the North-East region could be developed as a tourist haven by virtue of its topographic advantages, diverse cultures and its pristine areas unspoilt by pollution, tourism development has tended to elude it. The Plan expenditure incurred on the schemes operated in the North-East States has only been about 30 percent of the amount sanctioned during the first three years of the Ninth Plan. The concept of non-lapsable funds, introduced to ensure utilization of the funds, is meaningless if it does not translate into concrete development.

Convergence and Integration of Efforts: A Core Issue

Tourism sector is expected to grow and contribute significantly to the Indian GDP but cannot grow with the gaps in tourism infrastructural facilities. Success in a service industry and tourism in particular, depends to a large extent on better access to infrastructure, with a consumer-centric approach.

Core Issue: Infrastructure such as accommodation, restaurants, built attractions; and transport are primarily developed by the private sector. Private investors require good airport and road infrastructure and the availability of affordable basic services such as power, water, sewerage, electricity and telecommunications, making tourism investments economically viable.

It is a challenge for the Indian tourism to understand the dynamic global tourism scenario and have an active role of all stakeholders in development.

Human Resources Development and Capacity Building

The success of any industry depends to a great extent upon the quality of human resources and tourism is no exception. We have already learnt that tourism is a labour intensive industry which provides employment to skilled, semi-skilled and unskilled workers directly and indirectly. The progressive labour force with a dynamic management and responsive government and responsible society are the pillars of the tourism industry.

Traditionally, the employment has been seen as an area that is reactive to changes in the wide business environment. There is a widely accepted assumption that the role of people within organisations is required to change and develop in response to developments in markets, products and technology. Most of the large tourism companies recognized this assumption and have reorganised human resource functions such as training and development. This is possible only when the external labour market permits employers to adapt to these changing dimensions.

Development of Infrastructure

Ministry of Tourism has identified 21 circuits and 12 destinations for development. Financial assistance is provided to State/Union Territory (UT) governments for developing tourist infrastructure at these places. In the first three years of the Ninth Plan, 779 projects were taken up. It has been observed that many States, particularly in the North-Eastern region, could not avail themselves of the financial assistance provided under the scheme because they could not find the required matching contribution for projects prioritized under the scheme. There is a need for modifying the pattern of funding under the scheme to enable all such States to benefit from it. The scheme stipulates transfer of land ownership in respect of those projects in the name of the Central Government. The stipulation is acting as a deterrent in the operation of the scheme as the States face legal difficulties in transferring the land ownership.

Ministry of Tourism needs to take urgent action to waive the condition. The Ministry has envisaged an equity scheme for attracting funds from financial institutions but the scheme has not made much headway because the State governments have not been able to put up financially viable projects. There is a need to evaluate the scheme.

Destination Development

In tourism, destination region is perhaps one of the most important elements. Without the richness and variety of tourism environments around the world we would not have the same quality of tourist experience. In order to understand the essence of tourism, consideration has to be given to the different environmental, social and economic contexts around the world within which tourism destinations are located.

It is important for a destination to deliver quality experience and product, and in this regard, careful planning and management is essential to ensure a tourism industry based on sustainable development.

Thus, the stage is set for a range of new tourist destinations to be developed and effective management of the existing destinations. There is no doubt that these new and existing destinations need to be better planned and managed and show more concern for the environment and the host community. Accordingly, the Ministry of Tourism, Government of India has given a major thrust in this direction and is promoting tourism as a means for economic growth and social integration of the country. The role of government in tourism development has been redefined from that of a regulator to that of a catalyst. Apart from marketing and promotion, tourism development plan has to focus on an integrated development of enabling infrastructure through effective partnership with various stakeholders.

Suggestions for Development of Tourism

1. The success of tourism depends on the ability of the firms and destination to engage in sustainable use and conservation of vital resources. Destination development is the key to sustaining natural and cultural resources on which tourism depends. Therefore, steps have been taken up for the development of tourism destinations. The close interaction between the public sector, the destination's tourism marketing organisations, private sector and local residents in planning is the key principle of sustainable tourism. Thus, the stakeholders can work most effectively together to manage local-global influences on their natural and cultural resources. Effective destination development is an intricate problem faced by the tourism managers.
2. Although the North-East could be developed as a tourist haven by virtue of its topographic advantages, diverse cultures and its pristine areas unspoilt by pollution, tourism development has tended to elude it. The Plan expenditure incurred on the schemes operated in these States has been only about 30 percent of the amount sanctioned during the first three years of the Ninth Plan. The concept of non-lapsable funds, introduced to ensure utilization of the funds, is meaningless if it does not translate into concrete development.
3. The Approach Paper to the Twelfth Five Year Plan (2012-17), prepared by Planning Commission, highlights the need to adopt a 'pro-poor tourism' approach aimed at increasing the net benefits to the poor from tourism and ensure that tourism growth contributes to poverty

reduction. The approach paper also underpins the need to develop a comprehensive set of strategies for a diversity of actions, from macro to micro level, including product and infrastructure development, marketing, branding and promotion, planning, policy and investment.

4. The annual number of tourists should be regulated according to the carrying capacity of parks/hill resorts and other eco-sensitive zones after proper assessment of the carrying capacity of each region. Few world class carrying capacity studies in diverse areas should be carried out in each of the five years of the Twelfth Five Year Plan (2012-17). Tourism impact assessment must be made mandatory for any tourism project proposed to be undertaken in an eco-tourism zone with financial assistance from the Centre. State governments should be encouraged to evolve eco-tourism policies and set up eco-tourism boards to act as vehicles of eco-tourism policy deliverance. Gate receipts should flow back to the respective national parks and reserves in order to improve their protection and to facilitate their upkeep.
5. Some reasonable portion of revenue from tourism should be shared with local communities for common benefits. Local communities should also benefit directly from tourism through employment, promotion of local crafts, cuisine, home-stays, etc. Commercial activities permitted in eco-zones for facilitating tourists should preferably be entrusted to members of local communities. A fixed percentage, say 40 percent, of the employment in tourism establishments in eco-tourism zones should be reserved for the local communities.
6. National and international travel associations like TAAI, IATO, Eco Tourism Society of India, PATA, ASTA need to champion the cause of eco-tourism. Seminars, workshops and conferences should be undertaken for the stakeholders and NGOs to be involved in the process of local community/host community education/sensitisation.

7. For each eco-tourism site, a site specific association, which acts as watchdog for the welfare of wildlife and conservation, with tourism forest officials, NGOs and representatives of local communities should be set up.
8. For the development of heritage tourism:

- Surveys/studies should be undertaken in all States and Union Territories for: (a) collecting and compiling information on intangible heritage, (b) mapping the requirements of these heritages for planned development, and (c) preparing a list of all heritage sites and heritage buildings in association with state or national level organizations.
- A strategy should be evolved, in consultation with Ministry of Culture, NGOs and experts working for the protection and preservation of heritage sites, for inclusion of India's monuments and other heritage sites in the list of 'World Heritage Sites'.
- For all tourism projects undertaken at heritage sites with Central financial assistance, regulation of activities, like food and beverage services, light and sound shows, shopping, entertainment etc. in and around the sites must be made mandatory. Part of the funds generated at a site through these activities should be earmarked for maintenance and development of that site.
- Central and State Government offices in urban areas located in heritage buildings should be shifted and the buildings should be used for tourism related activities.
- All schools in the country should introduce a daily interactive session for students from class 5 onwards on waste management, basic hygiene, cleanliness, garbage disposal, energy and water conservation, discipline, first aid, road rules, etc. to inculcate civic sense and social responsibility among the young and impressionable children.
- Introduction of value addition services, including audio/video shows, automated audio guides, etc., at heritage sites

by States should be encouraged and financially supported by the Ministry.

- Capacity building programmes for guides at heritage sites should be intensified to increase the availability of qualified guides.
- At prominent heritage sites, part of gate receipts should go towards maintenance of the respective sites, as has been done in Rajasthan.

9. Tourism development should focus on developing tourism from people's perspective by involving local panchayats and local communities at various stages. This will help in understanding the social, cultural, and environmental impacts of tourism projects on local communities enabling the development of tourism in a sustainable manner. In addition, to realize the potential of the sector, the Ministry of Tourism should adopt a pro-poor approach aimed at increasing the net benefits to the poor from tourism and ensure that tourism growth contributes to poverty reduction. A wide range of actions are needed to increase the spread of benefits from tourism to weaker sections.
10. The Ministry of Tourism should provide funds to States/UTs for undertaking studies, through competent professional agencies, for identification and mapping of intangible heritage, including spiritual heritage. A study in each State should also be undertaken to list all heritage sites and heritage buildings in association with state or national level organisations.
11. The consumption demand, emanating from tourist expenditure, also induces more employment and generates a multiplier effect on the economy. As a result, additional income and employment opportunities are generated through such linkages. Thus, the expansion of the tourism sector can lead to large scale employment generation and poverty alleviation. The economic benefits that flow into the economy through growth of tourism in shape of increased national and State revenues, business receipts,

employment, wages and salary income, buoyancy in Central, State and local tax receipts can contribute towards overall socio-economic improvement and accelerated growth in the economy.

Conclusion

A perusal of the study has brought to light that tourism is one economic sector in India that has the potential to grow at an exponential rate and can ensure consequential development of the infrastructure of the destinations. It has the capacity to capitalize on the country's success in the services sector and provide sustainable models of growth. It has the potential to stimulate other economic sectors through its backward and forward linkages and cross-sectoral synergies with sectors like agriculture, horticulture, poultry, handicrafts, transport, construction, etc. Expenditure on tourism induces a chain of transactions requiring supply of goods and services from these related sectors. Therefore, the Government of India should continue to adopt policies that encourage travellers including a new visa regime, enabling investment in vital infrastructure, and developing a facilitating business environment. India is a beautiful and diverse tourism destination; with the right policies in place, it will no doubt continue to grow towards ranking even higher in terms of its tourism economy.

Endnotes

1. The Economist Intelligence Unit (EIU) is a British business within the Economist Group providing forecasting and advisory services through research and analysis, such as monthly country reports, five-year country economic forecasts, country risk service reports, and industry reports.
2. Compound annual growth rate (CAGR) is a business and investing specific term for the geometric progression ratio that provides a constant rate of return over the time period.
3. World Tourism Organisation (WTO) is the United Nation's agency managing promotion of responsible, sustainable and universally accessible tourism and its barometer ranks countries in terms of their international tourist arrivals (ITAs), comprising

both foreign tourist arrivals as well as non-resident arrivals.

References

Report of the Working Group on Tourism, Twelfth Five Year Plan (2012-17), Ministry of Tourism, Government of India, New Delhi.

www.assocham.org.

www.incredibleindia.org.

2

Growth and Performance of Indian Tourism Industry

Chidanand Patil and Chaitra G.B.

Introduction

United Nations has designated 2017 as the International Year of Sustainable Tourism for Development in its 70th General Assembly Meeting recalling the potential of tourism to advance the universal 2030 Agenda for Sustainable Development and the 17 Sustainable Development Goals (SDGs). The year 2017 is aimed to support a change in policies, business practices and consumer behaviour towards a more sustainable tourism sector that can contribute effectively to the SDGs.

The World Tourism Organization's Secretary General, Taleb Rifai opined, "This is a unique opportunity to build a more responsible and committed tourism sector that can capitalize its immense potential in terms of economic prosperity, social inclusion, peace and understanding, cultural and environmental preservation".

Tourism sector accounts for 7 percent of worldwide exports, 10 percent of the world's GDP and one in eleven jobs, and if the tourism sector is managed well, it can foster inclusive economic growth, social inclusiveness and protection of natural and cultural assets.

The International Year 2017 is aimed at promoting tourism's role in the five key areas namely, inclusive and sustainable economic growth; social inclusiveness, employment and poverty reduction; resource efficiency, environmental protection and climate change; cultural values, diversity and heritage; and mutual understanding, peace and security.

This paper examines the growth and performance of tourism industry in India while evaluating its contribution to employment generation in the country.

Tourism Industry in India

Among the services sector in India, tourism has emerged as one of the key driver of growth. Besides being an important source of foreign exchange for India, tourism is also a potentially large employment generator in India. Due to the rich cultural and historical heritage, variety in ecology, places of natural beauty which are spread across the nation, tourism sector has a significant potential in India.

Market Size: Rising middle class population and increasing disposable incomes in India have continued to support the growth of domestic as well as outbound tourism. As per the report of Ministry of Tourism, the domestic tourist visits to the States/Union Territories (UTs) grew by 15.5 percent year-on-year to 1.65 billion during 2016 and the top ten States/UTs contributed about 84.2 percent to the total number of domestic tourist visits.

During May 2017, the foreign tourist arrivals (FTAs) in India increased 19.5 percent year-on-year to 6,30,000 and FTAs on e-tourist visa increased to 68,000 with year-on-year increase of 55.3 percent.

According to the data of Ministry of Tourism, Government of India, the foreign exchange earnings (FEEs) of India through tourism increased by 32 percent year-on-year to reach US$ 2.278 billion in April 2017.

By 2030, India is expected to move up five spots to be ranked among the top five business travel markets globally and the business travel spending in the country is expected to treble from US$ 30 billion in 2015.

Investments: The tourism and hospitality sector is one of the sectors in India which attracts the highest foreign direct investment (FDI) among the top 10 sectors. According to the data released by the Department of Industrial Policy and

Promotion (DIPP), the hotel and tourism sector attracted around US$ 10.14 billion of foreign direct investment during the period April 2000 to March 2017.

Many companies have invested in tourism and hospitality sector in India due to the increased demand of global tourists towards tourism in India. In the year 2016, travel and tourism sector attracted a capital investment of ₹ 2,284.9 billion and it is anticipated to rise by 4.5 percent in 2017, and is expected to rise by 5.7 percent per annum over the next ten years.

Foreign Tourist Arrivals into India

Table 2.1 presents the foreign tourist arrivals into India for the period 2000 to 2017. The quantum leap of foreign tourist arrivals in India has increased from 2.65 million in 2000 to 8.80 million in 2016 and this has registered a positive significant compounded annual growth rate of 8.67 percent.

Between the years 2000 and 2016, the tourist arrivals into India barring the years 2001, 2002 and 2009 showed an increasing trend in absolute terms, but in relative terms, the percentage change in tourist arrivals showed an increasing annual growth rate of 8.67 percent. The decrease in foreign tourist arrivals to India during 2001, 2002 and 2009 may be attributed to political disturbances, global and domestic financial crisis and terrorism.

FTAs in India during the year 2010 were 5.78 million with a growth rate of 11.8 percent as compared to the FTAs of 5.17 million and growth rate of -2.2 percent during the year 2009. The major reason for growth rate in foreign tourists' arrival in the year 2010 can be attributed to Commonwealth Games organized by India.

During the last three years, the new government has launched several key projects as well as continued some old projects of the previous government to boost the travel and tourism sector. Among its top initiatives are Swachh Bharat, electronic visa, digital application, and Udan among others. The variation in arrivals of tourists in India during the study period was registered at 39.49 percent.

Table 2.1: Foreign Tourist Arrivals (FTAs) in India, 2000-2017

Year	FTA in India (in million)	Percentage change over the previous year
2000	2.65	
2001	2.54	-4.20
2002	2.38	-6.00
2003	2.73	14.30
2004	3.46	26.80
2005	3.92	13.30
2006	4.45	13.50
2007	5.08	14.30
2008	5.28	4.00
2009	5.17	-2.20
2010	5.78	11.80
2011	6.31	9.20
2012	6.58	4.30
2013	6.97	5.90
2014	7.68	10.20
2015	8.03	4.50
2016	8.80	9.70
CAGR	8.67 %	
CV	39.49 %	

Foreign Exchange Earnings from Tourism in India

Tourism sector is one of the important sectors of the Indian economy which contributes substantially towards country's foreign exchange earnings (FEEs). Table 2.2 depicts the FEEs from tourism in India during the period 2000 to 2016 along with the percentage change over the previous year. It is crystal clear that the foreign earnings have increased from US$ 3,460 million in 2000 to US$ 22,923 million in 2016 representing a positive and spectacular compounded annual growth rate of 14.24 percent. It indicates that the tourism industry in India has given continuous foreign exchange earnings to India. Higher instability was noticed in the quantum of FEEs from tourism in India.

Table 2.2: Foreign Exchange Earnings (FEEs) from Tourism in India, 2000-2016

(US$ million)

Year	FEE from Tourism in India	Percentage change over the previous year
2000	3,460	
2001	3,198	-7.60
2002	3,103	-3.00
2003	4,463	43.80
2004	6,170	38.20
2005	7,493	21.40
2006	8,634	15.20
2007	10,729	24.30
2008	11,832	10.30
2009	11,136	-5.90
2010	14,193	27.50
2011	16,564	16.70
2012	17,737	7.10
2013	18,445	4.00
2014	20,236	9.70
2015	21,071	4.10
2016	22,923	8.80
CAGR	14.24 %	
CV	56.76 %	

The "Incredible India" campaign which was launched in 2002 was one of the successful campaigns and its results were reflected in increase in the FEEs. International tourism receipts were stagnated at US$ 3103 million before the launch of Incredible India campaign and after its launch in 2002, FEEs increased to US$ 4,463 million in 2003 and during 2016 the FEEs from tourism stood at US$ 22,923 million. World Travel and Tourism Council says the travel and tourism contributes to 9.6 percent of the GDP and is expected to rise by 10 percent of the GDP in 2027.

Share of India vis-à-vis World and Asia-Pacific Region in International Tourist Arrivals

Table 2.3 denotes India's share of world tourist arrivals and Asia-Pacific Region for the period 2000 to 2016.

Table 2.3: Share of India in International Tourist Arrivals (ITAs) in World and Asia-Pacific Region, 2000-2016

Year	ITAs (in million)			Percent share and rank of India in World		Percent share and rank of India in Asia-Pacific	
	World	Asia-Pacific	India	Percent share	Rank	Percent share	Rank
2000	683.3	109.3	2.65	0.39	50	2.42	11
2001	683.4	114.5	2.54	0.37	51	2.22	12
2002	703.2	123.4	2.38	0.34	54	1.93	12
2003	691.0	111.9	2.73	0.39	51	2.44	11
2004	762.0	143.4	3.46	0.45	44	2.41	11
2005	803.4	154.6	3.92	0.49	43	2.53	11
2006	846.0	166.0	4.45	0.53	44	2.68	11
2007	894.0	182.0	5.08	0.57	41	2.79	11
2008	917.0	184.1	5.28	0.58	41	2.87	11
2009	883.0	181.1	5.17	0.59	41	2.85	11
2010	948.0	204.9	5.78	0.61	42	2.82	11
2011	994.0	218.5	6.31	0.63	38	2.89	9
2012	1039.0	233.6	6.58	0.63	41	2.82	11
2013	1087.0	249.7	6.97	0.64	41	2.79	11
2014	1134.0	264.3	13.11	1.15	24	4.86	8
2015	1184.0	278.6	13.28	1.12	24	4.67	7
2016	1235.0	308.7	14.57	1.18	25	4.72	8
CAGR %	3.95	6.72	11.57				
CV	19.77	32.48	63.20				

In absolute terms, the number of international tourist arrivals in the World and Asia-Pacific region has reached 1.8 and 2.8 times respectively but for India the number has increased to 5.5 times during the study period. The number of tourist arrivals in the world has increased from 683.3 million in 2000 to 1,235 million in 2016, registering a compounded annual growth rate of 3.95 percent. Fascinatingly, the number of international tourist arrivals in Asia-Pacific Region also increased from 109.3 million in 2000 to 308.7 million in 2016 with a positive and significant growth rate of 6.72 percent. Meanwhile, the number of international tourist arrivals into India increased from 2.65 million in 2000 to 14.57 million in 2016 recording a positive and remarkable growth rate of 11.57 percent.

Though India's share in international tourist arrivals was meagre compared to the Asia-Pacific Region, its share in the world tourist arrivals increased from 0.39 percent in 2000 to 1.18 percent in 2016 accounting for an impressive share of 4.72 percent of foreign tourist arrivals in the Asia-Pacific Region in 2016. India's rank in international tourist arrivals which was 50 and 11 in World and Asia Pacific Region in 2000 has improved to 25 and 8 respectively in 2016. The World Travel and Tourism Council state that India is one of the fastest growing tourism industries in the world and by 2027, is expected to support 4,98,68,000 jobs (9.6 percent of total employment), an increase of 2 percent per annum over the period. It is clear from Table 2.3 that the share of India in international tourist arrivals is continuously increasing in World and also in Asia-Pacific Region.

Source Countries for Foreign Tourist Arrival

Table 2.4 reveals that the majority of tourist arrivals are from Bangladesh followed by United States, United Kingdom and Canada. Share of Bangladesh, United States and United Kingdom in foreign tourist arrivals in India in 2016 was 15.68 percent, 14.73 percent and 10.70 percent respectively. The share of top ten countries in FTAs in India was 63.44 percent in 2016. The results indicate that the tourism industry in India is vibrant and considerably substantial and country is becoming a major global destination for tourism.

Contribution of Tourism Industry to Employment

Tourism sector plays a significant role both directly and indirectly in creating the job opportunities. The Indian government makes efforts to improve the employment opportunities in the tourism sector through international collaborations and by setting development plans. Total and direct contribution of travel and tourism industry to employment is represented in Table 2.5. Direct contribution to employment refers to the number of direct jobs within the travel and tourism industry whereas, total contribution to employment refers to the number of jobs generated directly in the travel and tourism industry plus the indirect and induced contributions.

Table 2.4: Source Countries for Foreign Tourist Arrivals in India in 2016

S. No.	Source Country	FTAs	Percent Share
1.	Bangladesh	13,80,409	15.68
2.	United States	12,96,939	14.73
3.	United Kingdom	9,41,883	10.70
4.	Canada	3,17,239	3.60
5.	Malaysia	3,01,961	3.43
6.	Sri Lanka	2,97,418	3.38
7.	Australia	2,93,625	3.33
8.	Germany	2,65,928	3.02
9.	China	2,51,313	2.85
10.	France	2,38,707	2.71
	Total Top 10 Countries	55,85,422	63.44
	Others	32,18,989	36.56
	Total	88,04,411	100.00

Tourism Infrastructure

Availability of good infrastructure is one of the essential requirements at selected tourist destinations. The infrastructure for tourism includes as under:

1. Travel infrastructure networks like airports, railways, roads, waterways, and telecommunications.
2. Amenities like electricity, water supply, drainage, sewerage, solid waste disposal systems.
3. Tourism facilities like accommodation, restaurants, recreational facilities, shopping malls, cable cars etc.

Table 2.5: Total and Direct Contribution of Travel and Tourism Industry to Employment, 2011-2017

Year	Total Job Opportunities ('000)	Total Real Growth (percent)	Direct Job Opportunities ('000)	Direct Real Growth (percent)
2011	36,928		23,358	
2012	37,328	1.07	23,508	0.64
2013	37,815	1.29	23,778	1.14
2014	38,812	2.57	24,352	2.36
2015	39,433	1.57	24,786	1.75
2016	40,343	2.26	25,395	2.40
2017	41,074	1.78	25,926	2.05
CAGR	1.86 %		1.83 %	

The operation of tourism facilities, services and amenities are often dependent on a number of travel infrastructure networks. The most usual case in tourism development is for infrastructure development to precede the completion of the tourism facilities. This means that the installation of the infrastructure becomes a public sector responsibility. The case for infrastructure services being a public sector responsibility is based on the consideration that the network of services is available to both tourists and residents of the area *and* the construction of an integrated system would also facilitate non-tourism development within the region.

The strategy for development of tourism infrastructure should essentially focus on identifying clusters of habitations/destinations having unique craft, ethnic art form, culture and heritage, natural spots for development as tourism products and development of tourist circuits/destinations around them with the active participation of local communities. As part of this strategy, State Governments should be expected to identify at least *one integrated tourist circuit*, map all the tangible and intangible natural and cultural assets along the circuit, estimate the sustainable destination carrying capacity and undertake a gap analysis of the travel infrastructure network and tourism facilities, services and amenities. Based on this, a comprehensive integrated physical and financial plan should be prepared through a community participatory process. The plan should identify, *inter alia*, the winners and losers, agencies responsible for executing the sub-components of the plan and the timelines for achieving the milestones. The integrated plan should be approved and monitored by the Ministry of Tourism.

Easy access to tourism destinations in terms of international transport and facilities for easy movement within the destinations are prerequisites for the development of tourism. India's ability to open up new areas and properly service emerging tourism resorts, while also providing access to natural tourism attractions and circuits for tours will significantly depend upon its ability to quickly improve the airport density and quality of rail and roads.

In terms of investment, especially private investment, tourist accommodation represents the most expensive facility in tourist resorts. In the past few decades, the character and composition of tourist accommodation has undergone considerable changes. New types of accommodation, such as self-catering units, home stay, budget hotel accommodation and camping sites, have evolved to meet market demands for increased levels of independence, self-sufficiency, informality, economy and convenience. Such changes have been influenced by the emergence of the new types of travellers and the tourists who invest in a holiday home or unit in a preferred tourism destination. As the spectrum of travellers has undergone transformation, there have also been changes in the requirements for traditional hotel accommodation.

The availability of hotel rooms in India is extremely limited. Further, there is an acute shortage of land in urban areas particularly in cities due to land market distortions. Therefore, the prospect of large-scale new traditional hotel accommodation is extremely limited. It is imperative to expand the number of registrations under the home stay scheme in various stays so as to significantly augment hotel room capacity in India. This will open up new livelihood opportunities for the local people.

Conclusion

Travel and tourism industry is one of the key sectors of the Indian economy leading the international trade in services and denoting the leading income activity for many parts of the country. Indian tourism industry is attracting many foreigners and showing a good growth, and has a vast potential for employment generation and earning large amount of foreign exchange as well as giving a boost to the country's overall economic and social development. Tourism sector in India should be improved in such a way that it entertains visitors in a way which is minimally destructive to the nature.

All wings of the Central as well as the State governments, voluntary organizations and private sector players must become active partners in the endeavour for attaining sustainable growth in tourism because tourism itself is a basically a service industry. Various events Cricket World Cup, Commonwealth Games and *Kumbh Mela* have contributed a lot to promote tourism in India. A policy implication which may be drawn from this study is that adequate measures must be initiated for maintaining the growth patterns of the Indian tourism industry. Through good forward and backward linkages between a host of sectors like hospitality, transport, health, agriculture, banking, education, etc., India can reap the full potential of this vibrant sector.

References

Kakkar, L. and Sapna (2012), "Impact of Tourism on Indian Economy", *International Journal of Marketing, Financial Services and Management Research,* 1 (4), pp. 70-75.

Kaur, M. and Sharma, N. (2012), "Growth and Development of Indian Tourism Industry", *Journal of Hospitality Application and Research,* 7 (2), pp. 14-24.

Padmasree, K. and Devi, B. (2011), "The Performance of the Indian Tourism Industry in the Era of Globalization: A Conventional Study', *African Journal of Hospitality, Tourism and Leisure*, 1 (4), pp. 1-5.

Patel, R. (2012), "India's Tourism Industry: Progress and Emerging

Issues", *Arth Prabhand: A Journal of Economics and Management,* 1 (5), pp. 1-10.

"Three Years of Modi Government: Tourism Sector", (2017, May 26), available at: http://businessworld.in/article/Three-Years-Of-Modi-Govt-Tourism-Sector/26-05-2017-119002.

"Tourism and Hospitality Industry in India", (n.d.), available at: https://www.ibef.org/industry/tourism-hospitality-india.aspx

World Tourism Organization (UNWTO) (n.d.), available at: http://media.unwto.org/press-release/2017-01-03/2017-international-year-sustainable-tourism-development.

3

Services Trade of India and Tourism

Parmjeet Kaur and Manpreet Kaur

Introduction

In global economy, tourism has appeared as a key sector and it has developed into a main labour force in world trade. In present economic scenario, it has been making an innovative and momentous impact on the whole economy of the world. Tourism has been identified as a major export industry in the world. The comprehensive nature of this business makes it a mechanism for economic progress and assists in balanced regional growth. It has provided big opportunity to earn foreign exchange at low social cost and because of this reason it is a low capital, labour intensive industry. Tourism trade plays a vital role for both economic and social change and it encourages employment and investment, change fiscal formation and makes positive contribution towards balance of payments. When tourists go to another country and spend the money in this process, the total income earned from tourism is number of times more than the real payments.

Regarding this process, the multiplier effect of tourism receipts is totally familiar as dispersal to secondary and tertiary areas of the economic actions of a country. In the context of tourism, marketing and promotion both are important because of the aggressive environment of the industry both within and between the countries. It creates direct, indirect and induced employment and creates a huge variety of employment from highly capable and skilled managers of five-star hotels to room boys, sales girls, and artisans. With the growth of this trade, new prospects of employment have opened up for the unemployed and underemployed youth of the developing countries.

Literature Review

Deardorff (2000) examined the special role that trade liberalization in service industries can play in stimulating not only trade in services itself, but also in enhancing gains from trade in goods. International trade in goods requires inputs from several services industries such as transportation, insurance, and finance in order to complete and facilitate international transactions. As a result, trade liberalization in services can yield benefits, by facilitating trade in goods, which are larger than one might expect from analysis of the services trade alone. The study also shows that, trade liberalization in services can also stimulate fragmentation of production of both goods and services, thus increasing international trade and the gains from trade even further.

Matto et al. (2001) in their study analysed measuring of services and trade liberalization and its impact on economic growth. Cross-country regression for a sample of 60 countries for the period 1990-99, concluded that services liberalization is different from trade in goods because the former involves factor mobility and leads to scale effects that are distinctive though not unique. Second, it is possible to construct policy-based rather than outcome-based measures of openness for the services sectors that capture these differences. Third, there is some econometric evidence relatively strong for the financial sector and less strong but nevertheless statistically significant for the telecommunications sector that openness in services influences long-run growth performance. Their estimates suggested that countries with fully open telecom and financial services sectors grow up to 1.5 percentage points faster than other countries. The authors suggested that the above results, however, need to be refined by incorporating more information in the construction of indices of openness and testing whether they hold for other services sectors too.

Mitra (2009) examined the impact of trade on services sector employment in India. These exercises have been pursued separately for four broad groups of services: trade and hotels, finance and business services, transport, storage and communication and community, social and personal services. Since there is no time series information on the informal service sector employment, NSS surveys on the informal sector employment for the years 1999-2000 and 2004-05 were considered and the cross-sectional information was used to examine the relationship between the formal and informal sectors. He suggested about the possibility of close links between growth and employment. He concludes that in the recent past, the acceleration in economic growth is able to translate itself into employment growth as well.

Chadda et al. (2010) assessed the growth, composition and comparative advantage of India's service trade for 27 years period from 1980 to 2007. Results suggest that services exports in the post-reform period have witnessed tremendous growth in transportation, travel and other commercial services. But it is the other commercial category which has led India's success story. Hence, these are the service categories where India needs to focus its attention. The change in the global scene and other economic and political factors are responsible for propelling the growth of India's service sector. India definitely has the right elements for becoming the preferred service provider as discussed in the present paper. This growth has helped India gain economic stability, confidence and respect at the international level. Now it is crucial to develop a long-term perspective.

Mukherjee (2012) recognized main number of obstacles faced by the services sector and suggests policy measures, which if implemented will lead to inclusive growth, increased productivity, generating quality employment, and increasing trade and investment. The methodology which is used in this study is based upon the RCA method. This study reveals that services sector is the fastest growing sector in India, contributing significantly to GDP, trade and FDI inflows. The share of services sector in India's total trade is higher than the global average and India is among the top 10 WTO member countries in services exports and imports. He concludes that India's export competitiveness is in a few services sector and there are wide variations in growth across different sub-sectors of services. Services sector faces a number of barriers, which makes it difficult for the sector to reach its full potential and contribute to inclusive growth. He suggested reform measures that will enable the services sector to not only grow at a fast pace but also create quality employment and attract investment.

Economic Growth and Global Tourism

In every society, tourism has been considered as a social phenomenon and it is influenced by the natural support of every human being for new experience, adventure, education and entertainment. The incentive for tourism also includes social, religious and business interests and it raises the knowledge to know more about different parts of the world. The essential human desire for new experience and education has grown to be stronger, as communication obstacles are getting overcome by technological advances. Due to progress of air transport and development of tourist services, it provides an optimistic vision for people to roam around the world.

For the development and growth of undeveloped and backward areas, tourism plays an important and significant role in the global economy. In terms of gross revenue and foreign exchange earnings, tourism also has an important concept. It can play a significant and successful role in attaining the growth with justice—goals which India has set for itself. In Indian economy, tourism trade is one economic sector that has the potential to produce at a high rate and can facilitate major development of the infrastructure sector for sustainable purposes. It also has the potential for growth of the sector through its backward and forward linkages and cross-sectoral synergies with sectors such as agriculture, horticulture, poultry, handicrafts, transport, construction etc.

In the case of tourism, direct employment multiplier is not

fairly high and direct employment of one person is estimated at 2.36 and in case of other sectors it is 1.36 due to linkages with tourism. These connections are in the following sectors, namely, agriculture horticulture, poultry, handicrafts, construction, sports etc. Regarding labour/capital ratio, it is very favourable in the tourism sector compared to various other industries with 47.5 jobs for a million rupee investment as has been seen in the survey conducted by the Ministry of Tourism (MoT), Government of India. Tourism sector encompasses private sector service in a substantial way, while the public sector has a considerable role to play in infrastructure areas either directly or through public-private-partnership (PPP) approach. The other related sectors include airlines, surface transport, hotels, basic infrastructure and facilitation systems, etc. Consequently, the growth of tourism cannot be attained unless the issues related to all the above sectors are addressed simultaneously.

Tourism also encourages maintenance of monuments and heritage properties and helps in the survival of arts forms, crafts and culture. It is also important to note that tourism has become an instrument for sustainable human development because it helps in creating jobs, reducing poverty, preserving the environment, and contributing to women empowerment.

Tourism in India

Tourism is a fairly large industry in India from various angles and contributes substantially to foreign exchange earnings and acts as a facilitator of employment opportunities. As we know, at the global level, India is the biggest democratic republic with enormous potential of expansion in the tourism sector. With its vast cultural and religious heritage and varied natural attractions, the country has an insufficient share in world tourism. It is a land of natural beauty having tropical weather to snowy mountains and depicts a diversity of rare natural and cultural endowments. It has plenty of natural beauty ranging from the towering Himalayas in the north to the sun-kissed beaches of the east and the breathtaking beauty of the west.

India has its own particular festivals, culinary culture and glorious tradition which are interlinked with the development of tourism in the country. According to great German scholar Max Muller, if we see the whole world scenario to find out the country most richly capable with all the wealth, power and beauty that nature can bestow it is India. The best tourist states in India include Uttarakhand, Rajasthan, Andhra Pradesh, West Bengal, Karnataka, Uttar Pradesh, Odisha and Haryana. Although India's share in international tourism is less than 0.4 percent, the tourism sector alone accounts for 5.8 percent of the total employment created in India. This sector contributes almost 5.6 percent of the national income.

Data and Methodology

The present study is entirely based on secondary data and covers the time-period from 2000 to 2013. The study mainly covers the period of second decade of globalization, i.e. 2000 to 2013. Limitation of the study is that data of India's services trade has been collected from 2000 to 2013. The study includes the secondary data from the following different sources. Data related to service trade is also obtained from the followingsources:

- Data for India's services trade has been collected from World Trade Organization (WTO).
- Data for India's trade in services performance,composition and direction have been compiled from World Trade Organization (WTO), United Nations Service Trade and International Trade Center (ITC).
- Data for calculation of different indices like revealed comparative advantage (RCA) and indicative export potential have been collected from World Trade Organization (WTO), United Nations Service Trade and International Trade Center (ITC).

Table 3.1 presents classification of major services in trade.

Table 3.1: Classification of Major Services in Trade

S. No.	SITC Code	Services
1.	205	Transportation
2.	236	Travel
3.	245	Communication
4.	249	Construction
5.	253	Insurance
6.	260	Financial
7.	262	Computer and information
8.	266	Royalties and license fees
9.	268	Other business services
10.	287	Personal, cultural and recreational
11.	291	Government services

Source: Based on Time Series Database, WTO, 2014.

The sources used for collecting information are United Nations Organization (UNO), World Trade Organization (WTO), Handbook of Statistics on Indian Economy and Reserve Bank of India. To analyze the data, the compounded growth rate has been calculated with the help of following formula and equation,

CAGR (%) = [logest (Yt1 + Yt2 +....Ytn)-1]*100

where,

Y= variable under study

t = time (1, 2.......n) for each period.

For analyzing competitiveness of India's exports, revealed comparative advantage (RCA) method developed by Balassa (1965) has been used.

The study selects India's major trade partners on the basis of their share in India's export and import of services trade during the period 2000-2017. These countries include Australia, Belgium, Germany, France, Italy, Japan, Malaysia, Singapore, South Korea, United Kingdom and the United States of America. The following indicators have been calculated and used to analyze the competitiveness.

Export Competitiveness: The degree of export

specialization of India with selected countries is calculated using the Balassa's revealed comparative advantage (RCA) for the average of years for the period 2000-2013 for particular services.

Revealed Comparative Advantage Index

Balassa's index (1965) of revealed comparative advantage (RCA) has been used to assess a country's export potential. A variation of his formula was further interpreted by Donges and Riedel (1977); Browen (1983) and Vollrath (1991). It is also more critically reviewed by Lapadre (2001). The index has been calculated at sector and services level using the SITC digit level classification. The RCA indicates whether a country is in the process of extending the services in which it has the export potential, as opposed to situation in which the number of services that can be traded with the new partners. Export competitiveness of individual service category will be calculated by revealed comparative advantage index given by Balassa (1965).

$RCA_{ij} = (X_{iJ}/X_{WJ}) / (Xi/X_W)$

Where, RCA_{ij}= revealed comparative advantage of the ith country's jth service.

Xij= exports of the jth service by the ith country.

X_i= total service exports of the ith country.

Xwj= world exports of the jth service.

X_j= total world exports of services.

RCA_{ij} ranges from (0) to ($+\infty$). A value of less than unity implies that the country has a less revealed comparative advantage in that service. Similarly, if the index exceeds unity, the country is said to have a stronger revealed comparative advantage in that service. If the value is equal to one, the country's specialization in a service is identical with the world specialization in that commodity (Balassa, 1977).

Overview of Performance of India's Tourism

Table 3.2 shows India's service trade with world for the

period 2000 to 2013.

Table 3.2: India's Trade in Services with World (US$ million)

Year	India's Trade			World's Trade		
	Exports	Imports	Trade Balance	Exports	Imports	Trade Balance
2000	22748 (1.04)	26692 (1.76)	-3943.34	21,89,660	15,19,090	6,70,570
2001	25630 (1.16)	28521 (1.85)	-2890.74	22,10,950	15,37,570	6,73,380
2002	28410 (1.19)	30805 (1.9)	-2394.57	23,89,090	16,22,800	7,66,290
2003	34991 (1.25)	36965 (1.98)	-1973.63	28,01,950	18,62,440	9,39,510
2004	66216 (1.95)	53173 (2.39)	13042.32	33,96,380	22,26,180	11,70,200
2005	92262 (2.42)	67450 (2.73)	24811.14	38,12,450	24,70,910	13,41,540
2006	124082 (2.85)	85520 (3.1)	38561.65	43,52,490	27,54,600	15,97,890
2007	154947 (2.94)	102569 (3.15)	52378.08	52,61,950	32,56,580	20,05,370
2008	191717 (3.25)	124447 (3.35)	67270.15	59,03,100	37,16,190	21,86,910
2009	160580 (2.94)	109189 (3.23)	51391.08	54,66,990	33,79,540	20,87,450
2010	197030 (3.31)	148486 (4.03)	48544.36	59,50,270	36,88,700	22,61,570
2011	230329 (3.43)	168107 (4.07)	62221.43	67,06,690	41,29,910	25,76,780
2012	250148 (3.64)	175072 (4.13)	75076.24	68,65,180	42,39,660	26,25,520
2013	265138 (3.65)	169294 (3.81)	95844.03	72,65,650	44,40,530	28,25,120
CAGR*	23.15	17.82		10.76	9.62	

Source: Calculated based on World Trade Organization (WTO), 2017.
*CAGR denotes compound annual growth rate.

In 2000, India's services trade improved from US$ 22748.73 million in 2000 to US$ 92262.11 million in 2005. In 2005, it reached at 2.42 percent mark, and by 2006 it reached 2.85 percent. This year witnessed the highest share of invisible exports in world exports. While India's imports of services from world increased from US$ 26692.07 million in 2000 to

US$ 67450.97 million in 2005, its percentage share also increased from 0.63 percent to 1.98 percent during the same period. Its trade balance remained in deficit from 2000 to 2003. Lack of adequate infrastructure, poor power supply, and high level of indirect taxes were main reasons for this trade deficit. Similarly, India's exports of services to world also increased at the growth rate 10.76 percent and its imports by 9.62 percent during the study period.

Table 3.3 depicts India's trade in travel with world from 2000 to 2013. India's export in travel increased from US$ 3459.88 million in 2000 to US$ 18395.79 million in 2013 at the growth rate of 16.42 percent. Similarly, in case of India's imports, it increased from US$ 2690.36 in 2000 to US$ 11570.83 million in 2013 at a growth rate 14.23 percent. The total trade increased at a growth rate 15.45 percent with overall trade balance found to be in surplus during the study period.

Revealed Comparative Advantage

Revealed comparative advantage is one of the most applied tools to measure the export competitiveness. It is defined as, "*the share of particular services in a country's total exports of the share of services in the world's total exports*". If the RCA is greater than 1, the country is said to have a comparative advantage in a particular service compared with rest of the world (Balassa, 1965).

Table 3.4 shows India's average of revealed comparative advantage of various export services with its major partners during 2000-2013. India has a great advantage with Australia in exports of services namely computer and information (1.34), followed by government services (0.70), and other business services (0.35). Similarly, India has a great advantage with Belgium in export of computer and information (15.2) followed by communication (8.16), transportation (4.50), insurance (4.25), and other business services (3.70). India has a great comparative advantage with Germany in terms of exports of services namely computer and information (17.3) followed by construction (8.46), government services (7.35), and other business services (6.73).

Table 3.3: India's Trade in Travel with World (US$ Million)

Year	Exports	Imports	Total Trade	Trade Balance
2000	3,459	2,690	6,150	7,692
2001	3,198	3,005	6,203	192
2002	3,102	2,988	6,090	113
2003	4,462	3,584	8,047	877
2004	6,169	4,815	10,985	1,353
2005	7,492	6,186	13,679	1,306
2006	8,633	6,844	15,478	1,788
2007	10,729	8,218	18,948	2,510
2008	11,832	9,606	21,438	2,226
2009	11,135	9,309	20,445	1,826
2010	14,489	10,489	24,979	4,000
2011	17,707	13,699	31,406	4,008
2012	17,971	12,341	30,313	5,629
2013	18,395	11,570	29,965	6,825
CAGR	16.42	14.23	15.45	27.80

*CAGR denotes compound annual growth rate.
Source: Calculations based on data provided by World Trade Organization (WTO), 2017.

On the other hand, India has a great extent of competitive advantage with France for government services (10.3) followed by computer and information services (7.71), and construction (6.73). During 2000-2013, India's had the highest revealed comparative advantage with Denmark in computer and information services (10.2) followed by government services (5.59), and transportation (4.67). Similarly, India again had a great extent of competitive advantage with Singapore for personal, cultural and recreational services (22.7), construction (12.9), other business services (7.14) and financial services (5.60). On the other hand, India had great revealed comparative advantage with Japan for personal, cultural and recreational services (21.6), followed by royalties and licence fees (3.76), financial services (3.43), and insurance (0.64).

Similarly, India had great export competitiveness with Sweden in other business services (3.48 percent), followed by computer and information (2.43 percent), and construction (2.26 percent). During 2000-2013, India had the highest comparative advantage with U.S.A. for travel services (3.10 percent), followed by computer and information (2.55 percent). Hence, it is clear that India has great competitive advantage in computer and information and other business services with partner countries.

Conclusion

Presently, trade in services has emerged as a prominent sector in the world economy. India's trade in services also plays a prominent role in world trade. Regarding services, trade tourism has appeared as a critical sector, and it has been making an innovative and considerable impact on the whole economic scenario.

Table 3.4: Revealed Comparative Advantage of India's Services (2000-2013)

(average share)

SITC Code	Name of Services	Australia	Belgium	Germany	France	Denmark
205	Transportation	-	4.50	4.44	4.93	4.67
236	Travel	0.33	2.21	-	4.09	1.36
245	Communication	-	8.16	3.95	2.68	1.51
249	Construction	-	3.02	8.46	6.73	2.68
253	Insurance	0.24	4.25	2.00	1.48	0.62
260	Financial	-	0.95	0.54	2.41	-
262	Computer and information services	1.34	15.2	17.3	7.71	10.2
266	Royalties and license fees	-	0.87	1.18	0.90	0.56
268	Other business services	0.35	3.70	6.73	2.81	2.46
287	Personal, cultural and recreational	0.10	-	-	1.65	0.18
291	Government services	0.70	-	7.35	10.3	5.59

Contd...

SITC Code	Name of Services	Japan	Singapore	Sweden	U.S.A	World
205	Transportation	0.50	4.20	1.78	1.02	0.54
236	Travel	0.27	-	-	3.10	0.53
245	Communication	0.26	-	1.70	-	1.17
249	Construction	0.09	12.9	2.26	-	0.44
253	Insurance	0.64	4.39	1.17	0.12	0.72
260	Financial	3.43	5.60	-	0.97	0.43
262	Computer and information services	0.06	-	2.43	2.55	7.21
266	Royalties and license fees	3.76	0.20	2.01	0.20	0.03
268	Other business services	0.21	7.14	3.48	-	1.31
287	Personal, cultural and recreational	21.6	22.7	-	-	0.51
291	Government services	0.69	-	2.15	1.36	0.50

Note: '-' Indicates that the either data was not available or there had been no export in the corresponding period.
Source: International Trade Centre (ITC) and United Nations Service Trade Statistics Database (2014).

It encourages services and assets and adds to the foreign exchange earnings and sustains the favorable balance of payment. For an economy, tourism facilitates critical sectors for economic, social, cultural, educational and political growth. India's exports of services to world have increased at a growth rate 10.76 percent and its imports at 9.62 percent during the study period. India's export in travel increased from US$ 3459.88 million in 2000 to US$ 18395.79 million in 2013 at a growth rate 16.42 percent. Its total trade has witnessed an increase at a growth rate of 15.45 percent. Overall, the trade balance has been found to be in surplus during the study period.

The results of revealed comparative advantage show that India's export competitiveness is in a few services and there are wide variations in growth across different sub-sectors of the services.

References

Balassa, B. (1965), "Trade Liberalisation and Revealed Comparative Advantage", The Manchester School, 33(2), pp. 99-123.

Balassa, B. (1977), "Revealed Comparative Advantage Revisited: An Analysis of Relative Export Shares of the Industrial Countries: 1953-1971", The Manchester School, 45(4), pp. 327-344.

Chanda, R. and Gupta, P. (2011), "Service Sector Liberalization in India: Key Lessons and Challenges", South African Institute of International Affairs Economic Diplomacy Programme, occasional paper no. 88.

Mitra, A. (2009), "Impact of Trade on Service Sector Employment in India", Institute of Economic Growth, University of Delhi, Delhi, working paper series no. E/298, 8(4), pp. 1-36.

World Trade Organization (2014), Time Series Database, available at:
https://stat.wto.org/Home/WSDBHome.aspx?Language.

Websites

http://shodhganga.inflibnet.ac.in/bitstream/10603/7806/4/04_chapter %201.pdf.

http://www.adb.org/sites/default/files/publication/30285/ewp-352.pdf.

http://citeseerx.ist.psu.edu/viewdoc/download?doi=10.1.1.17.3606&rep=rep1&type=pdf.

4

Tourism Industry in India: Gears and Glows

V. Palanisingh, V. Abdul Salahudeen and T.R. Gurumoorthy

Introduction

The Indian tourism and hospitality industry has emerged as one of the key drivers of economic growth and development of Indian economy among the services sectors in India. Tourism in India has significant potential considering the rich cultural and historical heritage, variety in ecology, and terrains and places of natural beauty spread across the country.

The Indian tourism industry is a large employment generator, besides being a significant source of foreign exchange earnings for the country. Tourism is a major engine of economic growth and an important source of foreign exchange earnings in many countries including India. It has a great capacity to create large-scale employment of diverse kind—from the most specialized to the unskilled and hence can play a major role in the creation of additional employment opportunities. It can also play an important role in achieving growth with equity.

The Ministry of Tourism has the main objective of increasing and facilitating tourism in India. The Government of India has identified niche products, to promote India as a 365 days destination, attract tourists with specific interest, and to ensure repeat visits for the unique products in which India has a comparative advantage. The niche products identified by the Ministry of Tourism include cruise, adventure, medical, wellness, golf, polo, meetings, incentives, conferences and expositions (MICE), eco-tourism, film tourism and sustainable tourism.

The Ministry of Tourism, Government of India permitted 100 percent FDI under automatic route for all construction development projects such as the construction of hotels and resorts, recreational facilities, and city and regional level infrastructure. In November 2016, the E-tourist Visa (e-TV) Scheme was launched under three sub-categories, i.e. e-tourist visa, e-business visa and e-medical visa. Prior to the launch of the scheme, the e-TV facility was available for 12 countries only. As of January 2017, 161 countries are covered under the scheme. This facility is now available at 16 airports and 5 major ports in the country. The e-tourist visa scheme has attracted a large number of tourists from countries like U.S., Germany and U.K. among others. There was a 142.5 percent increase in foreign tourist arrivals on e-visa in a year. Around 10.8 lakh tourists arrived on e-tourist visa in 2016 compared to 4.45 lakh in 2015. [1]

Tourism Products in India

Tourism in India has an impressive variety of tourism products:

- Heritage and culture tourism (with 26 world heritage sites).
- Eco-tourism (wild life in national parks).
- Adventure tourism (mountain climbing, mountain trekking, river-based sports including rafting).
- Wellness tourism (ayurveda and yoga institutes in Kerala and Rishikesh) and medical tourism (being developed by private sector hospital chains).
- Beach tourism (centred around Goa).
- Religious tourism (Varanasi, Haridwar, Tirupati, Bodh Gaya, Ajmer, Amritsar).
- MICE (meetings, incentives, conferences and exhibitions) tourism.
- Desert tourism.

- Rural tourism.

Undoubtedly tourism in India has a remarkable variety and contributes substantially to the economy, particularly in providing jobs—full time or part time. Growth in international tourist arrivals during the recent years has been significant. International tourism has also provided sustenance to the Indian handicrafts industry (carpets and other handcrafted textile products, brassware, inlaid marble and rosewood, bidri, paper mache etc).

Beaches are one of the most important destinations for the affluent tourists. India has a coastline of 6,000 kilometres but beach tourism is not well developed; Goa being the only international beach tourism destination in the country. One factor, which affects the competitiveness of beach tourism in India, is the stringent coastal regulations zone (CRZ) requirements, under which a hotel cannot be built within 200 metres of the coast. Such a restriction does not exist in any successful beach destination in the world.

Meetings, incentives, conferences and exhibitions (MICE) is another area of tourism in which India lacks in competitiveness because of lack of world class conference centre apart from Delhi's Vigyan Bhawan, which is normally reserved for government conferences.

Whether it is heritage tourism or beach tourism, the foreign tourists as well as domestic leisure travellers want some form of entertainment, particularly in the evening. For this purpose consideration needs to be given to allowing casinos to operate in certain locations. Though the subject has remained a taboo in the country it has to be borne in mind that casinos will not only increase the competitiveness of tourism destinations in the country but also have the potential to generate substantial revenues for the State Governments, just as lotteries have done for some of them. Casinos are the mainstay of the economies of tourist destinations such as Las Vegas, Monte Carlo and Macau. Singapore too has allowed the establishment of two casinos in its territory.

Medical tourism is an international dimension of the growth of the healthcare industry. Thailand has been able to attract more than 1 million medical tourists due to world class infrastructure facilities in Thailand. India should be able to replicate the Thailand example by focusing on development of good quality medical as well as tourism infrastructure. India certainly has the potential and the capacity to attract more than 1 million tourists per annum.

There are two clear advantages for India in the field of medical tourism. The first and the foremost is the cost advantage. The second unique advantage of India is that it offers holistic medicinal services. With yoga, meditation, *ayurveda*, allopathy and natural herbal treatments, India offers a unique basket of services to foreign patient-tourists that are difficult to match by other countries. Kerala has been the pioneering State in this area as evidenced by the fact that Kerala and *ayurveda* have virtually become synonymous with each other. The preference for health tourism in Kerala is so strong that Kerala Ayurveda Centre (KAC) has been established at multiple locations in various major cities.

Karnataka has also taken some very pioneering steps in promoting medical tourism. Government of Karnataka has planned to set up Bangalore International Health City Corporation in order to cater to international patients for a wide variety of healthcare products and treatments. The recent operations of children from Pakistan in Bangalore have not only helped boost the medical economy in the state, but also helped in fostering goodwill, peace and harmony between India and Pakistan.

In Maharashtra, there is a wide array of speciality and super-speciality hospitals that can help promote medical tourism. Some of the major hospitals already in the business of medical tourism are Lilavati Hospital, Jaslok Hospital, Breach Candy, Hinduja Hospital, Wockhardt Hospital and Apollo NUSI Wellness Retreat. The Asian Heart Institute at Mumbai's Bandra-Kurla Complex offers state-of-the-art facilities for all types of heart ailments. Hotels like Hyatt, JW Marriott, Renaissance and Resort offer extensive spa facilities for both domestic and international tourists.

Methodology

The secondary data has been collected from United Nations World Tourism Development Organisation (UNWTDO), India Tourism Statistics, India Brand Equity Federation of India (IBEF), World Travel Tourism Council and Ministry of Tourism, Government of India. Correlation analysis has been employed in SPSS package.

Review of Literature

Reeti Guptathe (2015), in his article "Tourism, FDI and Inclusive Growth in India" analysed the contribution of foreign direct investment (FDI) in facilitating tourism in India, pinpointed the challenges of tourism in India, and highlighted the issues that deserve the attention of policymakers for achieving inclusive growth through tourism sector.

G. Saravana Kumar and R. Krishna Raj (2015), in their paper "Status, Growth and Impact of Medical Tourism in India" analyze the status, growth and impact effects of medical tourism in complimenting the growth of hotel industry in India. The results show that there is a significant growth of medical tourism in India, which grew at the rate 30 percent in 2015. The standards of medical treatment and hospital facilities provided to patients have significantly improved in India with 21 hospitals in India already accredited by JCI. India holds 2nd rank in world's medical tourism sector. Globalization has further boosted the growth of medical tourism and it is found to be complimenting the growth of hotel and travel industry in India.

Shekhar Upadhyay (2016), in his paper "E-tourist Visa (ETV): A Medium of Attracting Tourists in India" investigates the phenomenon of e-tourist visa and also measures the impact of e-tourist visas on overall foreign tourist arrival during the time period 2014-15. It also lists out the challenges in implementing the e-visa facility on national security and other possible demerits of e-visa. Tourists in India have grown so much that introduction of such unique ways of attracting and facilitating foreign tourists became absolutely urgent and required.

Table 4.1 shows international tourist arrivals in India, world and Asia-Pacific region during the period 2010 to 2016. International tourist arrivals in India shows an increasing trend whereby it increased from 5.78 million in 2010 to 14.57 million in 2016, and registered a CAGR of 14.12 percent. Arrival of tourists in Asia-Pacific region simultaneously showed an increasing trend, advancing from 204.9 million in 2010 to 308.7 million in 2016 thereby registering a CAGR of 6.03 percent. World tourist arrivals also witnessed an increasing trend registering a CAGR of 3.85 percent. In terms of world tourism, India was ranked 25th in 2016; in Asia-Pacific region India was ranked 8th in 2016.

Table 4.1: Share of India in International Tourist Arrivals (ITAs) in World and Asia-Pacific Region, 2010-2016

Year	International Tourist Arrivals (in millions)			Percent Share and Rank of India in World		Percent Share and Rank of India in Asia-Pacific Region	
	India	Asia-Pacific	World	Percent share	Rank	Percent share	Rank
2010	5.78	204.9	948	0.61	42	2.82	11
2011	6.31	218.5	994	0.63	38	2.89	9
2012	6.58	233.6	1,039	0.63	41	2.82	11
2013	6.97	249.7	1,087	0.64	41	2.79	11
2014	13.11	264.3	1,134	1.15	24	4.86	8
2015	13.28	278.6	1,187	1.12	24	4.67	7
2016	14.57	308.7	1,235	1.18	25	4.72	8
CAGR (%)	14.12	6.03	3.85				

Source: Indian Tourism Statistics, 2017.

Table 4.2 reveals international check posts for foreign tourist arrivals in India. Delhi had the 1st rank for attracting foreign tourists to the tune of 2,617,304, followed by Mumbai at no. 2 with 1,522,987 tourist arrivals and 3rd rank being of Haridaspur with foreign tourist arrivals at 756,775, followed by Chennai check post, Bangalore check post, Kolkata and so on.

Table 4.2: Top 10 International Check Posts for Foreign Tourist Arrivals (FTAs) in India in 2016

International Check Post	Foreign Tourist Arrivals	Rank	Percentage Share
Delhi	2,617,304	1	29.73
Mumbai	1,512,987	2	17.18
Haridaspur	756,775	3	8.6
Chennai	717,363	4	8.15
Bengaluru	543,264	5	6.17
Kolkata	354,663	6	4.03
Cochin	315,663	7	3.59
Hyderabad	298,935	8	3.4
Goa (Dabolim)	279,322	9	3.17
Ahmedabad	194,836	10	2.21
Others	1,213,299	--	13.77
Total	8,804,411	--	100.00

Source: Indian Tourism Statistics, 2017.

Table 4.3 depicts source countries for foreign tourist arrivals in 2016. Bangladesh held the 1st rank with the arrival of 1,380,409 tourists with a share of 15.68 percent, followed by United States at no. 2 with the arrival of 1,296,939 tourists having a share of 14.73, and the 3rd rank was of United Kingdom with the arrival of 941,883 tourists having a share of 10.7 percent, followed by Canada, Malaysia, Sri Lanka and so on.

Table 4.4 shows the share of top 10 countries in world tourist arrivals in 2016. France occupied the 1st rank with the arrival at 82.6 million tourists and a share of 6.7 percent, followed by Unites States of America at no. 2 with the arrival at 75.6 million tourists and a share of 6.12 percent, Spain ranked 3rd with 7.4 million tourists and a share of 6.10 percent, followed by China, Italy, United Kingdom, Germany and so on. The arrival of India was 14.6 million and its share was 1.2 percent.

Table 4.3: Top 10 Source Countries for Foreign Tourist Arrivals (FTAs) in India in 2016

Country	Foreign Tourist Arrivals	Rank	Percentage Share
Bangladesh	13,80,409	1	15.68
United States	12,96,939	2	14.73
United Kingdom	9,41,883	3	10.7
Canada	3,17,239	4	3.6
Malaysia	3,01,961	5	3.43
Sri Lanka	2,97,418	6	3.38
Australia	2,93,625	7	3.33
Germany	2,65,928	8	3.02
China	2,51,313	9	2.85
France	2,38,707	10	2.71
Others	32,18,989		36.56
Total	88,04,411		100

Source: Indian Tourism Statistics, 2017.

Table 4.4: Share of Top 10 Countries of World Tourism Arrivals in 2016

(million)

Country	International tourist arrivals	Rank	Percentage share
France	82.6	1	6.7
USA	75.6	2	6.12
Spain	75.4	3	6.10
China	59.3	4	4.8
Italy	52.4	5	4.2
United Kingdom	35.8	6	2.9
Germany	35.6	7	2.9
Mexico	35	8	2.8
Thailand	32.6	9	2.6
Turkey	30.9	10	2.5
Total of top 10 countries	408.9		41.6
India	**14.6**		**1.2**
Others	705		57.2
World Total	1235		100

Source: Indian Tourism Statistics, 2017.

Table 4.5 shows the airport-wise arrivals on e-tourist visas in 2016. New Delhi Airport was ranked 1st with arrivals on e-tourist visa at 470,354 in 2016 and a share of 43.6 percent followed by Kolkata airport with e-tourist visa arrivals at 264,411 and a share of 24.4 percent, followed by Mumbai airport at no. 3 with e-tourist visa arrivals at 221,315 followed by Dabolim (Goa) airport, Chennai airport, Bangalore airport and so on.

Table 4.5: Major Airport-wise Arrival of Foreign Tourists Availing e-Tourist Visas during 2016 and January-June, 2017

Name of the Airport	2016	Rank	Percent Share	January-June, 2017	Percent Share
New Delhi	470,354	1	43.6	309,453	43.2
Mumbai	221,315	3	20.5	140,984	19.7
Dabolim (Goa)	103,536	4	9.6	77,027	10.7
Chennai	68,937	5	6.4	47,338	6.6
Bangalore	65,564	6	6.1	41,391	5.8
Kochi	39,909	7	3.7	25,175	3.5
Kolkata	264,411	2	24.4	17,488	2.4
Hyderabad	25,960	8	2.4	15,271	2.1
Trivandrum	16,730	9	1.5	10,928	1.5
Amritsar	14,865	10	1.4	10,408	1.5
Others	26,115		2.4	21,613	3
Total	1,079,696		100	717,076	100

Source: Indian Tourism Statistics, 2017.

Table 4.6 depicts international tourism receipts (ITRs) for the world and the Asia-Pacific region. World tourism receipts increased from US$ 931 billion in 2010 to US$ 1,220 billion in 2016 registering a CAGR of 3.94 percent.

In Asia Pacific region, it increased from US$ 255.3 billion in 2010 to US$ 366.7 billion in 2016 registering a CAGR of 5.31 percent. Foreign exchange earnings (FEEs) in India increased from US$ 14.19 million in 2010 to US$ 22.92 million in 2016 and it registered a CAGR of 7.09 percent. India was ranked 13th in world tourism receipts and 7th in Asia-Pacific region in 2016.

Table 4.6: International Tourism Receipts (ITRs) of India: 2010-2016

Year	International Tourism Receipts (in US$ billions)		FEEs in India (in US$ millions)	Percent Share and Rank of India in World		Percent Share and Rank of India in Asia-Pacific	
	World	Asia-Pacific		Percent Share	Rank	Percent Share	Rank
2010	931	255.3	14.19	1.52	17	5.56	7
2011	1042	289.4	16.56	1.59	18	5.72	8
2012	1117	329.4	17.73	1.59	16	5.38	7
2013	1198	360.2	18.44	1.54	16	5.12	8
2014	1252	359	20.23	1.62	15	5.64	7
2015	1196	349.5	21.07	1.76	14	6.03	7
2016	1220	366.7	22.92	1.88	13	6.25	7
CAGR	3.94	5.31	7.09	--	--	--	--

Source: Indian Tourism Statistics, 2017.

Table 4.7 shows domestic tourist visits in India in 2016.

Table 4.7: Domestic Tourist visits in India 2016

Rank	State/UT	Domestic Tourist Visits	
		Number	Percent Share
1.	Tamil Nadu	34,38,12,413	21.3
2.	Uttar Pradesh	21,17,07,090	13.1
3.	Andhra Pradesh	15,31,63,354	9.5
4.	Madhya Pradesh	15,04,90,339	9.3
5.	Karnataka	12,97,62,600	8
6.	Maharashtra	11,65,15,801	7.2
7.	Telengana	9,51,60,830	5.9
8.	West Bengal	7,44,60,250	4.6
9.	Gujarat	4,22,52,909	2.6
10.	Rajasthan	4,14,95,115	2.6
	Others	25,47,30,804	15.8
	Total	1,61,35,51,505	100

Source: Indian Tourism Statistics, 2017.

Table 4.8 reveals state-wise foreign tourist arrivals in India.

Table 4.8: State-wise Foreign Tourist Arrivals in India in 2016

State/UT	Foreign Tourist Arrivals in 2016		
	Number	Rank	Percent Share
Tamil Nadu	47,21,978	1	19.1
Maharashtra	46,70,048	2	18.9
Uttar Pradesh	31,56,812	3	12.8
Delhi	25,20,083	4	10.2
West Bengal	15,28,700	5	6.2
Rajasthan	15,13,729	6	6.1
Kerala	10,38,419	7	4.2
Bihar	10,10,531	8	4.1
Goa	6,80,683	9	2.8
Punjab	6,59,736	10	2.7
Total of top 10	2,15,00,719	--	87
Others	32,07,012	--	13
Total	2,47,07,732	--	100

Source: Indian Tourism Statistics, 2017.

Table 4.9 shows foreign tourist arrivals and foreign exchange earnings in India during the period 2010 to 2016. Foreign tourist arrivals in India increased from 17.91 million in 2010 to 24.71 million in 2016. In the year 2012, it decreased to 18.26 million and in the subsequent year witnessed an increasing trend, registering a CAGR of 4.71 percent. Foreign exchange earnings showed an increasing trend and increased from US$ 14.19 million in 2010 to US$ 22.92 million in 2016, registering a CAGR of 7.1 percent.

Table 4.10 depicts domestic tourist arrivals and per capita income in India. Domestic tourist arrivals in India witnessed an increasing trend and peaked from 747.7 million in 2010 to 1,613.55 million in 2016 thereby registering a CAGR of 11.6 percent. Per capita income in India increased from 1430.2 in 2010 to 1747.5 in 2016, registering a CAGR of 2.9 percent.

Table 4.9: Foreign Tourist Arrivals and Foreign Exchange Earnings in India

Year	Foreign Tourist Arrivals (in millions)	Percentage Growth Rate	Foreign Exchange Earnings (in US$ million)	Percentage Growth Rate
2010	17.91	---	14.19	---
2011	19.5	8.9	16.56	16.70
2012	18.26	-6.3	17.73	7.07
2013	19.95	9.2	18.44	4.00
2014	22.33	11.9	20.23	9.71
2015	23.33	4.4	21.07	4.15
2016	24.71	5.92	22.92	8.78
CAGR	4.71%	---	7.1%	---

Source: Indian Tourism Statistics, 2017.

Table 4.10: Domestic Tourist Arrivals and Per Capita Income

Year	Domestic Tourist Arrivals (in millions)	Percentage Growth Rate	Per Capita Income	Percentage Growth Rate
2010	747.7	---	1430.2	---
2011	864.53	15.63	1552.5	8.55
2012	1045.05	20.88	1514.8	-2.43
2013	1142.53	9.33	1504.5	-0.68
2014	1282.8	12.28	1600.9	6.41
2015	1431.97	11.63	1617.3	1.02
2016	1613.55	12.68	1747.5	8.05
CAGR (%)	11.6	---	2.9	---

Source: Indian Tourism Statistics, 2017.

Hypothesis Testing

1. Ho: There is no significant relationship between exchange rate and foreign tourist arrivals in India.

H1: There is a significant relationship between exchange rate and foreign tourist arrivals in India (Table 4.11).

Table 4.11: Hypothesis Testing 1: Correlations

		Exchange Rate	Foreign Tourist Arrivals
Exchange rate	Pearson Correlation	1	.900**
	Sig. (2-tailed)		0.006
	N	7	7
Tourist arrivals	Pearson Correlation	.900**	1
	Sig. (2-tailed)	0.006	
	N	7	7

**. Correlation is significant at the 0.01 level (2-tailed).

The correlation between exchange rate and foreign tourist arrivals is r = 0.900 and significant value is 0.006. This indicates that exchange rate and foreign tourist arrivals is not independent of each other. Here, the value of r = is 0.900 so it is considered to be a strong correlation.

2. Ho: There is no significant relationship between exchange rate and foreign exchange earnings in India.

H1: There is a significant relationship between exchange rate and foreign exchange earnings in India (Table 4.12).

Table 4.12: Hypothesis Testing 2: Correlations

		Exchange Rate	Foreign Exchange Earnings
Exchange rate	Pearson Correlation	1	.968**
	Sig. (2-tailed)		0.000
	N	7	7
Foreign exchange earnings	Pearson Correlation	.968**	1
	Sig. (2-tailed)	0.000	
	N	7	7

**. Correlation is significant at the 0.01 level (2-tailed).

The correlation between exchange rate and foreign exchange earnings is r = 0.968 and significant value is 0.000.

This indicates that exchange rate and foreign exchange earnings are not independent of each other. Here, the value of r is 0.968 and hence is considered to have a strong correlation.

3. Ho: There is no significant relationship between government spending, capital investment and foreign tourist arrivals.

H1: There is significant relationship between government spending, capital investment and foreign tourist arrivals (Table 4.13).

Table 4.13: Hypothesis Testing 3: Correlations

		Capital Investment in Tourism	Foreign Tourist Arrivals
Capital investment in tourism	Pearson correlation	1	.934**
	Sig. (2-tailed)		0.002
	N	7	7
Tourist arrival	Pearson correlation	.934**	1
	Sig. (2-tailed)	0.002	
	N	7	7

**Correlation is significant at the 0.01 level (2-tailed).

The correlation between capital investment in tourism and foreign tourist arrivals is r = 0.934 and significant value is 0.002. This indicates that capital investment in tourism and foreign tourist arrivals are not independent of each other. Here, the value of r is 0.934 so it is believed to have a strong correlation.

Conclusion

The tourism sector is one of the fastest growing and emerging sectors in India. In India, we have rich cultural and historical heritage, variety in ecology, terrains and places of natural beauty spread across the country. 100 percent FDI is permitted under automatic route; e-visa facility and visa on arrival are the facilities which will further boost the Indian tourism sector. International tourist arrivals in India have seen an increasing trend, jumping from 5.78 million in 2010 to 14.57 million in 2016, registering a CAGR of 14.12 percent.

Foreign exchange earnings from tourism in India increased from US$ 14.19 million in 2010 to US$ 22.92 million in 2016 achieving a CAGR of 7.09 percent. India was ranked 13th in world tourism receipts and 7th rank in the Asia-Pacific region in 2016. Tamil Nadu was the topmost state in the country in terms of domestic tourist arrivals at 34,38,12,413 with a share of 21.3 percent in total domestic arrivals.

Endnote

1. http://www.makeinindia.com/sector/tourism-and-hospitality accessed on October 10, 2017.

References

Dayananda, K.C. and Leelavathi, D.S. (2016), "Tourism Development: Economic and Employment Growth in India", *Journal of Humanities and Social Science*, Vol. 21, Issue12, pp. 35-40.

Ganesh, Aurobindo and Madhavi, C. (2007), "Impact of Tourism on Indian Economy: A Snapshot", *Journal of Contemporary Research in Management*, Vol. 1, No. 1, January 2, pp. 235-240.

Gupta, Reeti (2015), "Tourism, FDI and Inclusive Growth in India", *Pacific Business Review International*, Vol. 7, Issue 12, pp. 100-114.

Irfan, M. and Yadav, A.K. (2016), "Travel in India': International Advertising Programme for Promoting Multi-Dimensional Tourism in India", *Journal of Tourism Hospitality*, Vol. 5, Issue 2, pp. 2-8.

Jaiswal, Dinesh K. and Jaiswal, Mona (2016), "A Review Analysis on Reforms: New Visa (e-Tourist Visa) Policy to Encourage FTAS in India", *International Journal of Science and Research*, Vol. 5, Issue 3, pp. 159-165.

Kakkar, Leena and Sapna, P. (2012), "Impact of Tourism on Indian Economy", *International Journal of Marketing, Financial Services and Management Research*, Vol. 1, No. 4, pp. 70-75.

Mahalakshmi, Venkatesh P., Joseph, Stanley and Raj, Michal (2016), "Impact of Tourism in India", International Journal of Scientific

Engineering and Applied Science, Vol. 2, Issue 1, pp. 168-184.

Padmasree, K. and Bharathi Devi, Anchula (2011), "The Performance of the Indian Tourism Industry in the Era of Globalization: A Conventional Study", *African Journal of Hospitality, Tourism and Leisure*, Vol. 1(4), pp. 1-4.

Upadhyay, Shekhar (2016), "E-tourist Visa (ETV): A Medium of Attracting Tourists in India", *Abhinav National Monthly Refereed Journal of Research in Commerce & Management*, Vol. 5, Issue 3, pp. 8-17.

Upadhyay, Shekhar, Awasthi, Alka and Rawal, Priyanka (2017), "A Comparative Study on Foreign Tourist Arrivals in India", *International Journal of Application and Innovation in Engineering and Management*, Vol. 6, Issue 4, pp. 17-24.

5

Incredible India Campaign: Opportunities and Challenges for Tourism

Prashant H. Bhagat

Introduction

The Ministry of Tourism has the main objective of increasing and facilitating tourism in India. Augmenting tourism infrastructure, easing of visa regime, assurance of quality standards in services of tourism service providers, etc. are some of the responsibilities of the Ministry.

The Ministry of Tourism, as part of its ongoing promotional activities, releases campaigns in the international and domestic markets under the 'Incredible India' brandline, to promote various tourism destinations and products of India to increase foreign tourist arrivals and domestic visits within the country. A series of promotional activities are undertaken in important and potential markets overseas through the India Tourism offices abroad and within India through domestic India Tourism offices, with the objective of showcasing India's tourism potential to foreign and domestic tourists.

An Incredible India Tourism Investors Summit was organized at the Vigyan Bhawan, New Delhi from September 21-23, 2016 with the objective of positioning the Indian tourism sector for attracting large investments. As on February 6, 2017, the State Governments of Chattisgarh, Gujarat, Karnataka, Rajasthan and Uttarakhand have signed 86 MoUs for developing tourist places in their respective states. The 5th International Buddhist Conclave was organized in Delhi, Varanasi, Sarnath and Bodhgaya from October 2-6, 2016 by the Ministry of Tourism, Government of India, in collaboration with the State

Governments of Uttar Pradesh and Bihar.

This paper focuses on the concept of Incredible India campaign and the opportunities and challenges associated with this campaign. In line with this objective, the study is based on the secondary data available from standard research in tourism sector, Ministry of Tourism, Government of India Annual Reports, articles etc.

Incredible India

Incredible India is a marketing campaign launched by the Government of India in 2002 to promote India as a tourist destination internationally. In 2012, India Tourism launched two new campaigns: Find What You Seek, an international campaign; and Go Beyond, a domestic campaign. In 2013, the Ministry of Tourism had welcomed the launch of a campaign '777 Days of the Indian Himalayas' as a step to promote the Himalayan states as well as the gateway cities which are entry points for domestic and international tourists. In 2015, the Ministry of Tourism launched new TV advertisement campaigns through which four films have been made on the theme of *Adithi Devo Bhava* which spreads awareness that conveys on how to extend hospitality by adopting friendly attitude towards tourists visiting India.

The activities of this Ministry revolve around promoting internal tourism, i.e. both inbound and domestic tourism, in India. This is necessary in order to harness the direct and multiplier effects of tourism on employment and poverty eradication in the country. The other major objectives of the Ministry pertain to projecting the country as a 365 days' tourist destination, promoting tourism in a sustainable manner by active participation of all segments of the society, assuring quality standards amongst tourism service providers, etc. Apart from these, the focus is also on integrated development of tourism infrastructure and facilities through effective partnership with various stakeholders. The role of Government in tourism development has been redefined from that of a regulator to that of a catalyst and requires synergy and convergence with different stakeholders.

Major Components of Incredible India Programme

Incredible India Bed and Breakfast/Homestay Scheme: The scheme offers foreign and domestic tourists an opportunity to stay with an Indian family and enjoy the warm hospitality and get a taste of Indian culture and cuisine in a clean and affordable place. With a view to encourage the growth of such establishments and also to simplify the procedure of approvals, this Ministry has reviewed the scheme and has simplified the guidelines.

E-Visa: The Ministry of Tourism has been working very closely with the Ministry of Home Affairs and Ministry of External Affairs for easing of the visa regime in the country over a period of time. As per Ministry of Home Affairs/ Foreigners Divisions' Circular No. 482 dated December 29, 2016, e-visa is allowed under three sub-categories, i.e. e-tourist visa, e-business visa and e-medical visa. Following activities will be permitted under e-tourist visa, e-business visa and e-medical visa:

- **e-Tourist Visa:** Recreation, sightseeing, casual visit to meet friends or relatives, and attending a short-term yoga programme.
- **e-Business Visa:** All activities permitted under normal business visa as per the visa manual.
- **e-Medical Visa:** Medical treatment, including treatment under Indian systems of medicine.

Multilingual Tourist Infoline

The Ministry of Tourism has setup a tourist infoline/ contact centre to provide information services and also guide the tourists during any emergencies such as medical, crime, natural calamities or on being stranded etc. This service is available on toll free number 1800111363 or on a short code 1363. The tourist infoline service will provide a sense of security to tourists who can contact the Government for guidance/information during emergencies while travelling in India and also seek tourist information etc. This facility is available in Hindi, English and 10 other languages namely Arabic, French, German, Italian, Japanese, Korean, Chinese, Portuguese, Russian, and Spanish.

Outdoor Publicity

For greater visibility of Incredible India, outdoor advertising campaigns including advertising at airports and on buses/trams, hoardings and billboards have been undertaken at prominent places in the important cities including Finland, Denmark, Paris, Barcelona, London, Los Angeles, Vancouver, Toronto, Venice, Moscow, Tokyo, Busan, Seoul, Sendai, Korea, Nagoya, Kyoto, Roppongi, Taipei City, Osaka, Taiwan, Daegu, Singapore, Rome, Milan, Thailand, Malaysia, Abu Dhabi, Sydney, Canberra, Perth, Melbourne, Adelaide, Brisbanc etc.

Food Festivals

For promotion of the Indian Cuisine, which is an integral component of the Indian tourism product, support has been extended to Indian food festivals by sponsoring Indian chefs for the food festivals in many countries. To celebrate important events and exhibit the fineries of gastronomy, various food festivals and promotions were organised. Some of these are:

- Navratra Food Festival, Shahi Gulnaar Festival and Biryani and Shorba Festival at Hotel Janpath, New Delhi.
- Biryani and Kebab Festival at Hotel Kalinga Ashok, Bhubaneswar.
- Kebab and Sizzler Promotion at Hotel Jammu Ashok, Jammu.

Familiarization Tours under the Hospitality Programme

One of the important elements of the marketing strategy and plan of this Ministry is the hospitality programme, under which this Ministry invites travel writers, journalists, photographers, film/TV teams, travel agents and tour operators, agencies promoting incentive/convention travel, opinion makers/dignitaries/celebrities/speakers and door prize/contest winners, through the India Tourism offices overseas, to effectively project India as an attractive multidimensional tourist destination offering a vast range of attractions. These invited guests are able to get first hand information/knowledge of the Indian tourism products during their familiarization tours.

Swachha Bharat Abhiyaan

A project monitoring unit (PMU) under Swachh Bharat Mission set up in the Ministry of Tourism is mandated to discharge the following functions:

1. To serve as the secretariat for the Swachh Bharat Abhiyan/Campaign Clean India.
2. To assist in formulation of strategies related to Swachh Bharat Abhiyan/Campaign Clean India.
3. Monitoring and inspection of initiatives pertaining to cleanliness.
4. Collection, compilation, analysis and publication of statistical data specific to cleanliness.
5. Interaction with the other Ministries, States/UTs and the stakeholders through appropriate means including meetings.

Integrated Development of Tourist Circuits around Specific Themes—Swadesh Darshan

Swadesh Darshan scheme has a vision to develop theme based tourist circuits on the principles of high tourist value, competitiveness and sustainability in an integrated manner by synergizing efforts to focus on needs and concerns of all stakeholders to enrich tourist experience and enhance employment opportunities.

Under Swadesh Darshan scheme, following thirteen

thematic circuits have been identified:

- North-East India Circuit.
- Buddhist Circuit.
- Himalayan Circuit.
- Coastal Circuit.
- Krishna Circuit.
- Desert Circuit.
- Tribal Circuit.
- Eco Circuit.
- Wildlife Circuit.
- Rural Circuit.
- Spiritual Circuit.
- Ramayana Circuit.
- Heritage Circuit.

During 2016-17, Ministry of Tourism sanctioned 31 projects under the Swadesh Darshan scheme.

National Mission on Pilgrimage Rejuvenation and Spiritual Augmentation Drive (PRASAD)

This Scheme is proposed to be implemented in a Mission Mode. The main mission objectives and strategy are as under: Integrated development of pilgrimage destinations in a planned, prioritized and sustainable manner to provide complete religious tourism experience; Follow community based development and pro-poor tourism concept in development of the pilgrimage destinations.

Heritage Hotels

The popular concept of heritage hotels was introduced to convert the old palaces, havelis castles, forts and residences built prior to 1950, into accommodation units that reproduce the ambience and lifestyle of the bygone era. Such hotels are categorized under three categories viz. heritage, heritage classic, and heritage grand based on the standards of facility and services as per the applicable guidelines. With effect from December 16, 2014, a new category of heritage hotel i.e. heritage classic (without alcohol scrviccs) has been introduced.

Challenges

Servicing the tourism Sector with skilled manpower effectively is a pre-requisite for the actualization of tourism specific expectations. This is both an imperative and a challenge. The task of creating a skilful service is inherently challenging for two reasons: first, because of the huge skill gap that exists in the tourism Sector, and second, because the tourism sector is not averse to taking raw hands and leaving them to acquire function-related skills on the job.

One of the main challenges and one which is still being debated, despite the success of the Incredible India campaign, is the best strategy to market brand India. The general opinion among the Indian travel trade is that India should come up with 20 best brands or destinations to attract overseas tourists instead of promoting the entire country through the Incredible India campaign.

The best way to lessen the complexity of India is to build brands. This way they will find it easy to market India. At the moment, there is no specific thrust. This tends to confuse tourists. State governments could also highlight the best feature of their state like mountains, trekking, beaches, wildlife or just ayurveda, religion, culture and heritage. India has so many things to offer, that we need to market properly.

It makes a lot of sense to create different brands which will help travellers easily identify a site. At the moment, tourists grope in the dark when they see different tourist sites being publicized. Many states feel that their unique positioning is lost out in an umbrella branding and have been running their own marketing and branding campaigns at times, not even linking themselves to the Incredible India campaign. It is not unusual for Indian travel trade members visiting major travel trade shows like WTM, ITB Berlin.

Another major hurdle for Incredible India Mission is the lack of adequate infrastructure. Most countries in the world are recording growth in their tourism sector on account of rise in disposable incomes, liberalization of international airspace, low cost carriers and the use of internet as a travel tool. Many Indian travel service providers feel that inbound figures may dip on account of lack of quality infrastructure, especially in accommodation.

While India is witnessing a lot of activity in the hospitality sector with a flurry of international hotel chains entering the market, there are a number of challenges faced by the hospitality players. Finding a suitable location for setting up a hotel due to acute shortage of land is the biggest challenge faced by the industry.

The other challenge would be its acquisition. With all the legalities and the formalities involved, it becomes quite a cumbersome task to acquire land and get approval for construction. Apart from that there is a major shortage of skilled manpower, which is a scrious concern in the country. The costs involved in setting up a hotel are much higher in the Indian market as compared to others.

Establishing India as a year-long destination for leisure travel is also another challenge. India is being recognized as both, a business and a leisure destination. The contribution of the government has been significant: the open sky policy, privatization of airports and improvement in rail and road connectivity. But a challenge that the industry is facing is to establish India as a year-long destination for the international leisure travellers. Tour operators, hotels, airlines, state tourism boards and other tourism players must work together to bring about this change in perception.

Opportunities

1. Creating awareness among the local communities about the importance of tourism for them in terms of increase in sources of income, improved living standards and overall development of the area.
2. Enhancing the tourist attractiveness in a sustainable

manner by developing world class infrastructure in the circuit destination.

3. Harness tourism potential for its direct and multiplier effects in employment generation and economic development.
4. To identify and prioritize projects that need to be taken up through dedicated public funding immediately and to leverage to the extent feasible, additional resources from voluntary funding (corporate social responsibility) initiatives of central public sector undertakings and the corporate sector.
5. Enhancing the tourist attractiveness in a sustainable manner by developing world class infrastructure in the religious destinations.
6. To identify religious destinations that have potential to be showcased as world class tourism products in consultation with the stakeholders.
7. To plan in an integrated manner, the development of these destinations in a specific timeframe ensuring full convergence of state and central government schemes as well as private sector investments.
8. Wellness tourism is about travelling for the primary purpose of achieving, promoting or maintaining maximum health and a sense of well-being. It is about being proactive in discovering new ways to promote a healthier, less stressful lifestyle or finding balance in one's life. Health tourism holds immense potential for India. The Indian systems of medicine, that is ayurveda, yoga, panchakarma, rejuvenation therapy, etc., are among the most ancient systems of medical treatment in the world. India can provide medical and health care of international standards at comparatively low cost. Most of the hotels/resorts are coming up with ayurveda centres. The leading tour operators have included ayurveda in their brochures.
9. India Tourism offices overseas have participated in major

international travel fairs and exhibitions in important tourist generating markets the world over as well as in emerging and potential markets to showcase and promote the tourism products of the country.

10. As India prepares to launch Incredible India 2.0 with a budget of over US$ 46 million, it will need to determine its message to the world, define its audience, and forge partnerships to ensure its success. It should also take a step back and consider how India is described by tourists who have travelled to India.

Impediments to Tourism in India

Paucity of tourist accommodation, inadequate transportation arrangements made expensive by deficient infrastructure and taxation, inadequate development of tourist destinations, which are bereft of ambience and lacking in amenities for tourists and facilities for their entertainment are some of the major impediments. One aspect that is becoming increasingly relevant is the sheer shortage of places of entertainment within a motorable distance of cities where families may go for leisure purposes for weekends. Most of the hill stations in both North and South India are highly overcrowded during the season and is avoided by the tourist class that has a large disposable income. There are other more specific problems also and we take them all up in turn.

Air Transport: A few years ago, non-availability of seats on flights to and from India deterred international tourists and the high domestic fares were a handicap for leisure travellers within the country. The position has eased considerably and with the progressive liberalization of bilateral agreements and introduction of open skies policy, there is better availability of seats on international flights. The process of liberalization must continue in order to increase: (a) direct international connectivity with non-metro destinations and (b) direct air connectivity with long haul overseas markets. The entry of low cost domestic carriers has improved access to air travel within the country as well and eventually could lead to opening up new areas to tourism in India such as the North-East.

Road Transport: A large number of foreign and domestic tourists use dedicated tourist vehicles mainly buses for visiting tourist destinations and the private sector has made large investments in these vehicles. The road and passenger tax regimes of the State Governments increase the cost of travel but more importantly they are a source of harassment for the tourists because of the manner of their implementation. Some States charge taxes on a quarterly basis, some per day and others on a per seat basis, which could be in addition to the quarterly charges. The buses carrying tourists have to stop at the borders for long periods on every trip as the papers are checked and taxes collected where necessary. Even if the quarterly or daily taxes have been paid there is no respite from standing in the queue along with other such vehicles and trucks. The problem is exacerbated by the limited and over worked staff.

Maintenance of Heritage Sites: The Archaeological Survey of India (ASI) has the responsibility for the maintenance and upkeep of all monuments and archaeological sites notified by the Government of India as a protected monument under the Ancient Monuments and Archaeological Sites and Remains Act, 1958. Some of the States have also enacted similar legislation and notified monuments and archaeological sites under the Acts. The allocation of funds made available to the ASI is grossly inadequate for the maintenance and restoration of the monuments and the environs of these monuments. The difference that adequate funds can make to a monument has been well illustrated by the case of Humayun Tomb in New Delhi, which has been transformed with the help of donations from the Agha Khan Foundation. Paucity of funds is also a contributory factor for the present state of neglect in which the Delhi Red Fort finds itself. The position is not very different in the case of monuments protected by the State Governments. In a large number of monuments not even minimum facilities such as provision of drinking water and toilets has been provided.

Suggestions

Building Demand for Tourism: To enable India to increase its international arrivals and continue to generate employment opportunities to reach nearly 50 million new positions (or 9.6 percent of the country's jobs) by 2027, emphasis should be placed on boosting demand for India as a destination. To do so, it is essential to create stimulating value propositions, foster a tourist-friendly environment and brand the country as a destination by discovery.

Creating Adequate Supply for Travel and Tourism: While emphasis should be placed on increasing the demand for India as a tourist destination, it should be complemented with the development of adequate supply. To do so, investing in infrastructure is necessary, from airports to roads and hotels to tourist service infrastructure, as is focusing on implementing progressive legislations and ensuring digital infrastructure throughout the eco-system.

Investing in an Enabling Environment: To make India a tourism hotspot, creating a powerful narrative and developing a distinctive experience is not enough. India must establish an enabling environment for business development for both domestic and foreign investment. Emphasis should be put on ensuring that India's environment supports the development of the industry.

Training the Talent: Over the last decade, the term "demographic dividend" has been used repeatedly to describe India's burgeoning youth population, which will be instrumental to the next wave of economic growth. By 2020, India will be the world's youngest country with an average age of 29 years. This youth bulge will only be a demographic dividend if the country invests in the education and skills of its citizens and ensures they gain meaningful employment.

Conclusion

The Incredible India campaign, launched 15 years ago, was extremely successful in raising awareness about India as a destination. The campaign was beautiful and its slogan was memorable. Yet, as the government considers how to promote India for the coming years, an externally facing campaign should only be part of the solution.

Incredible India 2.0 should not just be a marketing campaign, but part of a holistic approach to Indian tourism. In effect, as India markets its destination, it needs to make sure that it delivers on its promises to international visitors namely, providing a safe, seamless, connected and unique experience. Yet, to do so, it is essential to prioritize travel and tourism through progressive policies and set clear targets for the country to achieve.

Bringing together business and government to define smart targets will be critical to ensure that the entire industry can coalesce and be held accountable to ambitious targets and their achievement. Targets could range from increasing international arrivals to 20 million by 2030 and domestic demand to 200 million by the same date, to creating 30 million new jobs by 2030 and adding 30 Indian destinations as hotspots. Without prioritizing the industry and committing to bold and measurable targets, India will have little incentive to make the necessary adjustments to unlock its potential and deliver high-quality experiences to its travellers.

Today, empty promises from brands and destinations alike puts countries and companies at risk of bad publicity, which they may have difficulty recovering from. Indeed, creating a mismatch between traveller expectations and experiences will result in negative word of mouth publicity, which in turn will be amplified by travel review sites and social media.

References

Bain and Company (2017), "Tourism Opportunity for India", Draft Discussion Document Prepared for the World Economic Forum, September.

India Brand Equity Foundation (IBEF) (2017), "Tourism and Hospitality", January.

Ministry of Tourism, "Annual Reports, 2012 to 2017".

World Travel and Tourism Council (2017), "India is the World's 7th Largest Tourism Economy in Terms of GDP", Press Release, April 4.

6

Global Emergence of Agri-tourism: Implications for India

Manpreet Kaur and Naresh Singla

Introduction

Agriculture and allied sectors play an important role in India as around 54.6 percent of Indian population is engaged in this sector though its share in gross domestic product (GDP) has declined to 14.6 percent. Unfortunately, at present, farming has become an unprofitable enterprise mainly for marginal and small farmers who collectively occupy around 85 percent of the operational landholdings in India. Farm income of the farmers has reached almost a plateau due to stagnation in productivity of crops, creeping rise in price of inputs, rising cost of cultivation, inefficient marketing system of agriculture in terms of delay in procurement of crops, fluctuations in prices of non-MSP (minimum support price) crops etc. Hence, the financial conditions of farmers are becoming miserable in India. Diversifying farming from agricultural production to other viable farm enterprises may act as boon for supplementing the farm incomes. Agri-tourism, in this context, may emerge as an area for compensating from unprofitable agricultural production system and generating additional income for farmers.

Meaning and Definitions of Agri-tourism

The term *agri-tourism* appeared during the early twentieth century. However, it has achieved familiarity among the farmers, visitors and consumers of agricultural products as well as services in the recent years and is also predicted to continue expanding in future. The meaning of this term has been studied with a lot of contexts and methods. But, there is no universal accepted definition of agri-tourism; rather it is a very complex and complicated phenomenon. Hence, agri-tourism comprises a large number of on-farm activities that forms the educational and recreational base for the tourists. Three characteristics of agri-tourism activities include: type of farm (working or non-working); nature of contact between the farmers and visitors (passive, indirect or direct) and authenticity of contact (authentic or staged). On the basis of these characteristics, five class typology of agri-tourism was also developed later.

1. **Non-working Farm (NWF) Agri-tourism:** It refers to the activities whereby the ex-farm house is served its services for tourist purposes. In other words, it indicates accommodation in a farm house where agricultural activities form the basis of tourist products e.g. horse riding in a converted farm.
2. **Working Farm Passive Contact (WFPC) Agri-tourism:** In this type of agri-tourism, the current operating working farms provide tourist facilities to visitors. However, the activities of the tourists do not require much interaction with hosts or farmers on farm worksite. Their (farmers) job is just limited to providing tourists accommodation and food; e.g. wedding in a vineyard.
3. **Working Farm Indirect Contact (WFIC) Agri-tourism:** It involves operations for tourists that are related to on-farm activities with greater emphasis on enjoying agricultural products rather than doing the practice of farming by the visitors themselves e.g. enjoying the taste of fresh farm produce.
4. **Working Farm Direct Contact Staged (WFDCS) Agri-tourism:** This includes activities in which visitors experience various farming activities. Farming demonstrations is the best example of WFDCS agri-tourism.
5. **Working Farm Direct Contact Authentic (WFDCA) Agri-tourism:** In this type of agri-tourism, tourists

themselves experience physical farm operations. They do various on-farm activities such as picking the fruits, milking the cows etc. Hence, tourists contribute their labour services in farm operations in exchange of food and accommodation.

However, there is a revised typology of agri-tourism by replacing the term *contact with interaction*, merging passive contact into indirect interaction and thereby, distinguishing only direct and indirect interaction. It also categorises the non-working farm into two categories viz.

1. **Non-working Farm Indirect Interaction Agri-tourism (NWFII):** It comprises of non-working farm locations such as accommodation and other tourism activities (like horse riding) performed in farm house properties.
2. **Non-working Farm Direct Interaction Agri-tourism (NWFDI):** It includes products that are based on off-farm locations such as model farms, agricultural shows and agricultural sales mart. Hence, the visitors are engaged in off-farm and ex-farm settings for a better presentation of agricultural heritage.

As per World Tourism Organisation, agri-tourism is the activities of persons travelling to and staying in places outside their usual environment for not more than one consecutive year for leisure, business and other purposes not related to the exercise of an activity remunerated from within the place visited.

Rural Tourism vs. Agri-tourism

Before moving forward towards the scope of agri-tourism, it is important to recognise the difference between rural tourism and agri-tourism. Sometimes, rural tourism and agri-tourism has been used interchangeably. These two terms are not identical to each other, rather these two are strongly interlinked with each other. Rural tourism is a broader concept and a multi-faceted activity that takes different forms in different parts of the world. Rural tourism is based on rural amenities such as rural culture, rural folk, religion etc. in general, whereas agri-tourism is based on particular activities performed at farms. Hence, agri-tourism is a subset of rural tourism.

Agri-tourism Practices at International Level

History of agri-tourism goes back to late 1800s when families visited farming relatives in order to escape from the chaos of cities. Along with the use of automobiles, visiting the country became more popular in the 1920s. Hence, rural recreation gained consideration in the 1930s and 1940s for getting rid from the stresses of the Great Depression and World War II. Consequently, these rising demands for rural recreation led to extensive popularity in horseback riding, farm petting zoos and farm nostalgia during the 1960s and 1970s. Further, farm vacations and farm tours were commercialised in the 1980s and 1990s.

Agri-tourism Activities Performed by Various Countries

Agri-tourism involves a wide range of agricultural practices such as farming, fishing, bee keeping, poultry, dairying, forestry, processing of agricultural products etc. that are visited or experienced by the visitors for their recreation, knowledge and interest. However, these activities differ across country to country depending upon the major agricultural practices performed by the farmers of those countries. In the United States, this enterprise is developing at a very fast pace and offers a large series of tourism activities ranging from tours to wineries to wildlife observation and festivals. The visitors visit for educational, recreational self-harvest and leisure purposes. For recreational self-harvest tourists, visitors are provided services such as picking fruits and vegetables, and experiencing agricultural processes like cider mill etc. In case of educational activities, they participate in classes, seminars, workshops, animal displays etc.

Hence, the U.S. agri-tourism sector provides a diverse spectrum of services. In Thailand, agri-tourism is developed due to the expansion of floriculture and horticultural crops which include ornamental plants, flowers, vegetables, local fruit, shiitake mushrooms and handicrafts. Tourists also purchase fresh farm produce from the roadside stalls. Agri-tourism is seen as widely spread across European countries and its activities cover experience of all the farm operations as well as trade in agricultural commodities. Besides this, accommodation and hospitality are important parts of agri-tourism.

It has also proved as a significant tool for women empowerment in France as women rear sheep for milk and at the same time, these play a massive role in growth of agri-tourism. Agri-tourism is a worldwide phenomenon and it has been fully developed in Italy as in Italy, tourists are provided overnight stays, food, product tasting, lodging, horseback riding, hiking, naturalistic observation, sports in terms of mountain biking and educational activities etc. Besides, the enterprise has proved environment friendly and has contributed significantly in putting positive impacts on landscape, biodiversity and natural resources. In developing countries such as Nepal and Sri Lanka, the enterprise of agri-tourism is also growing.

However, from the review of above studies, it may be concluded that the business of agri-tourism is better developed in Western countries such as United States and United Kingdom as compared to developing Asian countries. In Singapore, agri-tourism is concentrated towards fisheries, livestock, horticulture and agriculture. The potential of agri-tourism is fully exploited in California farms as tourists have different options for enjoying the farm life while picking peaches, playing in corn mazes, shopping at on-farm produce, holding wedding in farms and vineyard etc. In this context, the different activities are enjoyed as well as performed by agri-tourists all over the world on the basis of different types of potentials to exploit agri-tourism.

Impact of Agri-tourism on Farmers

Linking agriculture with tourism has proved beneficial for the farmers for farm diversification as well as for generating additional incomes. The tourism sector in Norway has expanded so much that some family members doing off-farm jobs have quit their jobs and are now involved full time in tourism business. It has improved the livelihoods as well as local agricultural occupation of farmers in southern Thailand through the demonstration of product processing, agricultural study, product distribution, and agri-business guidance. Agri-tourism also provides better marketing linkages for selling of agricultural products in Thailand. It creates a direct trade between producers and consumers and hence, farmers get better prices than selling it in the open market and thereby, are also not exploited by middlemen. Selling directly to tourist consumers also saves their cost of transportation.

Besides generating income from recreation activities, agri-tourism also brought revenue from the selling of farm products. In addition to playing a significant role in generating additional income, agri-tourism is also seen as creating positive external effects for the non-agricultural sectors in Thailand as along with purchasing farm products, visitors also bought non-farm products from the villages. As a consequence, it has also resulted in development of micro and small enterprises in villages for such activities like craft production and food and drink stalls. Agri-tourism has also become beneficial for educational purposes as it cannot only help in educating those who are preparing for the field experiences, but also help those who wish to seek knowledge of rural areas, traditional rural art and culture.

Diversification of agriculture towards agri-tourism has also changed the social identity of the farmers in Norway. Visitors were having strong preference towards rural based activities in Israel. Apart from providing benefits to farmers, it is also an important source of public education and awareness regarding various agricultural practices. Hence, visitors also benefit from working farm direct staged interaction as well as working farm direct authentic interaction types of agri-tourism. Participation in agricultural tasks through WFDAI also somehow fulfils the labour requirement and the visitors also contribute towards farm economy. Small Islands have also positive impact on agri-tourism as it has transformed a small scale and farmer-oriented activity to a larger scale activity accompanied mainly by various professionals (including farmers) combining different services and integrating the agri-tourism experience with other tourism products.

Despite having various benefits of agri-tourism, there are also some constraints of agri-tourism. Agri-tourism is Sri Lanka is not well-developed rather it is in initial stages. Its activities are performed by limited number of hands at different scales. Further, these operators are outsider non-farmers and thereby the opportunities of rising farm incomes by developing agri-business are exploited by non-farming communities leaving no betterment to farmers. From the supply side, lack of awareness among farmers regarding agri-tourism, financial constraints, lack of proper management skills, no guidance and lack of motivation are the major reasons for thin participation of farmers in agri-tourism. However, from the demand side, low numbers of visitors, poor infrastructure and lack of publicity are considered as reasons for passive growth of agri-tourism in Sri Lanka. In this context, access to farm credit, proper training and education to farmers and proper measures for waste management may solve the issues and challenges associated with agricultural tourism in Sri Lanka.

Agri-tourism in India

In India, the concept of agri-tourism emerged in 2005. In 2005, an entrepreneur Pandurang Taware founded Agri Tourism Development Corporation (ATDC) to promote and facilitate agricultural tourism in Maharashtra state in order to generate employment opportunities and raise community income through small business development and local entrepreneurship by expanding the market base for local businesses. It operates agri-tourism centre by encouraging more farmers to take up agri-tourism and conducts training and research programs. In 2007,

ATDC launched training and skills development programs under the Maharashtra State Agri-tourism Vistar Yojana. Initially, 52 farmers were selected in Maharashtra.

However, it has not developed across all the Indian states. Undoubtedly, India has a vast potential to raise farmers' incomes and diversify their farm operations by expanding agri-tourism. However, in India, agri-tourism has not received as much attention and support from government bodies as it deserves. Therefore, India is lagging behind the Western economies in case of agri-tourism development. As a consequence, a very few studies have been conducted in India on agri-tourism as it has not developed as much as it needs to be. However, developing agri-tourism has various positive implications for India.

1. In India, share of agriculture in gross domestic product is continually declining. The emergence of agri-tourism may act positively to fight against the falling share of agriculture in GDP.
2. In India, agriculture is no more a viable enterprise in a majority of states. Productivity of various crops has stagnated and cost of cultivation is rising year by year. Despite all these issues, around 50 percent of population is engaged in agriculture and allied activities. Therefore, the enterprise of agri-tourism has the potential to generate the gainful employment for working force in agriculture by shifting them away from traditional agriculture to emerging agri-tourism.
3. Land is the most significant factor of production in agriculture. However, the supply of land is perfectly inelastic. Therefore, in India, around 85 percent of the operational landholdings belong to small and marginal farmers but they operate only 45 percent of the area. Therefore, along with the abundant family sizes and tiny pieces of land, it has become difficult to meet both ends with traditional agricultural production. Linking agriculture with tourism may act as a boon to pull them from the clutches of poverty.
4. Linking agriculture with tourism also has an important

implication for Indian agricultural marketing system as marketing of various agricultural commodities follows traditional practices and involves a large number of intermediaries. Therefore, producer's share in consumer's rupee falls too much. With the help of agri-tourism, visitors will directly come in contact with farmers and may purchase a variety of farm products. Therefore, it may be beneficial for the expansion of innovative marketing channels.

5. At present, the cropping pattern in India is mainly concentrated towards food grain crops. The main agricultural leading states such as Punjab, Haryana, Uttar Pradesh etc. are facing various negative impacts of rice-wheat monoculture. Farmers are still not ready to shift area from these crops to other less water consuming and horticultural crops which are demanding at peak level as no other crop covers their risks due to fluctuations in prices of other crops. However, with the emergence of agri-tourism, they may easily shift the area from these traditional crops to other high value crops as due to increasing awareness for health and food patterns, the tourists may demand for healthy food basket comprising of fruits and vegetables even at high prices. Since in agri-tourism, farmers themselves determine the prices of their products without any government regulations as well as in the absence of market functionaries, they will be able to earn better prices than food grain crops. It will also be beneficial from the consumers' or tourists' point of view as they have to pay more than double the price than farmers' selling price in the market. Purchasing directly from farmers will also be economical for them.
6. Shifting agriculture towards tourism may also expand area under organic farming as most of the educated and urbanised population understands the nutritional value of organic products. Farmers directly do not shift area towards organic farming as there are some drawbacks in

the marketing of organic products. But, through direct marketing system between the farmer and the visitor at higher prices from farm gate, will reduce the transaction costs on the one hand and will expand area under organic farming on the other which will further be helpful in maintaining the environmental sustainability.

7. From the macro point of view, with the development of agri-tourism in India, farmers may become price makers instead of price takers as the enterprise may reduce government interventions and marketing agents at the mandi levels. Consequently, the income levels of farmers may increase significantly.

Hence, from these positive implications of agri-tourism in India, it may be concluded that the enterprise of shifting agriculture towards tourism is a profitable business for farmers, visitors and also for the government.

Conclusion

It is clear that agri-tourism is well-developed in Western economies and it has been able to upgrade the livelihoods of farmers and enhance their income levels. It also acts as a significant tool for creating self-employment and poverty reduction. Visitors enjoy and participate in various agricultural practices. It has opened the doors for research in the areas of rural art, folk and agronomy as well. However, in developing countries like India, it has not grown as much as it should have except Maharashtra. In India, the emergence of this type of tourism may have some positive implications such as rising incomes and employment, reducing poverty, crop diversification, promotion of organic farming and hence, environmental sustainability, emergence of innovative marketing channels etc. Apart from these implications, the business of agri-tourism can be explored in India as it has the potential for it in terms of rising urbanisation, increasing literacy level and increasing keenness to understand the rural as well as the agricultural system.

Moreover, India is also a leading country in foreign tourists' arrivals. Therefore, government and policy makers should welcome this new type of tourism in India and make every possible effort to check the various threats such as poor infrastructural facilities in terms of roads, railway, banking, ATMs, IT, Wi-Fi etc. Besides this, most of the Indian farmers are not aware about the concept of agri-tourism. In this regard, government should take initiatives through media, programmes, camps etc. for creating awareness among farmers as it will be beneficial both for the farmers in terms of raising their income levels and for Indian economy in terms of earning foreign exchange reserves.

References

Annes, A. and Wright, W. (2015), "Creating a Room of One's Own': French Farm Women, Agri-tourism and the Pursuit of Empowerment", *Women's Studies International Forum,* 53, pp. 1-11.

Arroyo, C.G., Barbieri, C. and Rich, S.R. (2013), "Defining Agri-tourism: A Comparative Study of Stakeholders' Perceptions in Missouri and North Carolina", *Tourism Management,* 37, pp. 39-47.

Badrinath, V., Agalya, A., Abirami, G., Aarthi, M. and Aishwarya, R. (2016), "Scope for Promoting Agriculture-cum-Rural Tourism in Thanjavur District: A Case Study", *Indian Journal of Science and Technology*, 9(27), pp. 1-8.

Brandth, B. and Haugen, M.S. (2011), "Farm Diversification into Tourism: Implications for Social Identity", *Journal of Rural Studies*, 27, pp. 35-44.

Bruch, M.L. (2005), "An Introduction to Agri-tourism", Agri-tourism in Focus: A Guide to Tennessee Farmers, The University of Tennessee.

Busby, G. and Rendle, S. (2000), "Transition from Tourism in Farms to Farm Tourism", *Tourism Management*, 21, pp. 635-642.

Choenkwan, S., Promkhambut, A., Hayao, F. and Rambo, A.T. (2016), "Does Agro-tourism Benefit Mountain Farmers? A Case Study in Phu Ruea District, Northeast Thailand", *Mountain Research and Development*, 36(2), pp. 162-172.

Choo, H. and Petrick, J.F. (2014), "Social Interactions and Intentions to Revisit Agri-tourism Service Encounters", *Tourism Management*, 40, pp. 372-381.

Clarke, J. (1999), "Marketing Structures for Farm Tourism: Beyond the Individual Provider of Rural Tourism", *Journal of Sustainable Tourism*, 7(1), pp. 26-47.

Delfino, C. (2014), "A Case Study on Apple Hill Grower's Association: An Agri-tourism in Camino, CA", doctoral dissertation, California Polytechnic State University, San Luis Obispo, USA.

Doke, A. (2016), "Agro-tourism is an Emerging Field of Sustainable Development for Rural Area: A Case Study of Bhor Tahsil of Maharashtra", *International Research Journal of Multidisciplinary Studies*, 2(1), pp. 1-11.

Dubois, C., Cawley, M. and Schmitz, S. (2017), "The Tourist on the Farm: A 'Muddled' Image", *Tourism Management*, 59, pp. 298-311.

Flanigan, S., Blackstock, K. and Hunter, C. (2014), "Agri-tourism from the Perspective of Providers and Visitors: A Typology-based Study", *Tourism Management*, 40, pp. 394-405.

Flanigan, S., Balckstock, K. and Hunter, C. (2015), "Generating Public and Private Benefits through Understanding what Drives Different Types of Agri-tourism", *Journal of Rural Studies*, 41, pp. 129-141.

Fleischer, A., Tchetchik, A., Bar-Nahum, Z. and Talev, E. (2018), "Is Agriculture Important to Agri-tourism? The Agri-tourism Attraction Market in Israel", *European Review of Agricultural Economics*, pp. 1-24.

Government of India (2015), "Agricultural Statistics at a Glance", Department of Agriculture, Co-operation and Farmers' Welfare, Ministry of Agriculture and Farmers' Welfare, Government of India, New Delhi.

Government of India (2015-16), "Annual Report", Department of Agriculture, Cooperation and Farmers' Welfare, Ministry of Agriculture and Farmers' Welfare, Government of India, New Delhi.

Hausler, N. and Kasuske, D. (n.d.), "Back to the Roots: Agri-tourism in India", *International Case Studies in Sustainable Travel and Tourism*, pp. 135-137.

Henderson, J.C. (2009), "Agro-tourism in Unlikely Destinations: A Study of Singapore", *Managing Leisure*, 14(4), pp. 258-268.

Ilbery, B., Bowler, I., Clark, G., Crockett, A. and Shaw, A. (1998), "Farm-based Tourism as an Alternative Farm Enterprise: A Case Study from the Northern Pennines, England", *Regional Studies,* 32(4), pp. 355-364.

Karampela, S., Kizos, T. and Spilanis, I. (2016), "Evaluating the Impact of Agri-tourism on Local Development in Small Islands", *Island Studies Journal*, 11(1), pp. 161-176.

Karri, G.N. (n.d.), "Scope of Agri-tourism in India (With Special Reference to Development, Challenges, Extension and Advisory Services)", master's project, National Academy of Agricultural Research Management Rajendranagar, Hyderabad, India.

Kumbhar, V. (2009), "Agro-Tourism: A Cash Crop for Farmers in Maharashtra (India)", MRPA Paper No. 25187.

Lupi, C., Giaccio, V., Mastronardi, L., Giannelli, A. and Scardera, A. (2017), "Exploring the Features of Agri-tourism and its Contribution to Rural Development in Italy", *Land Use Policy*, 64, pp. 383-390.

Malkanthi, P. and Routray, J. (2011), "Agri-tourism Development: The Case of Sri Lanka", *ASEAN Journal of Hospitality and Tourism*, 10, pp. 3-16.

Malkanthi, P. and Routray, J. (2011), "Potential for Agri-tourism Development: Evidence from Sri Lanka", *The Journal of Agricultural Sciences*, 6(1), pp. 45-58.

Mastronardi, L., Giaccio, V., Giannelli, A. and Scardera, A. (2015), "Is Agri-tourism Eco-friendly? A Comparison between Agri-tourism and Other Farms in Italy Using Farm Accountancy Data Network Dataset", *Springer Plus*, 4(1), p. 590.

Na Songkhla, T. and Somboonsuke, B. (2012), "Impact of Agro-tourism on Local Agricultural Occupation: A Case Study of Chang Klang District, Southern Thailand", *Journal of Agricultural Technology*, 8(4), pp. 1185-1198.

Nilsson, P.A. (2002), "Staying on Farms: An Ideological Background", *Annals of Tourism Research*, 29(1), pp. 7-24.

Ollenburg, C. and Buckley, R. (2007), "Stated Economic and Social Motivations of Farm Tourism Operators", *Journal of Travel Research*, 45(4), pp. 444-452.

Parkar, P. (2015), "Developing Agri-tourism in Ratnagiri District of Konkan (Maharashtra): Issues and Challenges", *Online International Interdisciplinary Research Journal*, 5(2), pp. 145-152.

Petroman, I., Varga, M., Constantin, E.C., Petroman, C., Momir, B., Turc, B. and Merce, I. (2016), "Agri-tourism: An Educational Tool for the Students with Agro-food Profile", *Procedia Economics and Finance*, 39, pp. 83-87.

Phillip, S., Hunter, C. and Blackstock, K. (2010), "A Typology for Defining Agri-tourism", *Tourism Management*, 31, pp. 754-758.

Sharpley, R. and Vass, A. (2006), "Tourism, Farming and Diversification: An Attitudinal Study", *Tourism Management,* 27, pp. 1040-1052.

Rilla, E., Hardesty, S.D., Getz, C. and George, H. (2011), "California Agri-tourism Operations and their Economic Potential are Growing", *California Agriculture*, 65(2), pp. 56-65.

Slavic, I.P. and Schmitz, S. (2013), "Farm Tourism Across Europe", *European Countryside*, 4, pp. 265-274.

Srisomyong, N. and Meyer, D. (2015), "Political Economy of Agri-tourism Initiatives in Thailand", *Journal of Rural Studies*, 41, pp. 95-108.

Sznajder, M., Przezborska, L. and Scrimgeour, F. (2009), "Agri-tourism", Oxfordshire, UK: CAB International.

Tew, C. and Barbieri, C. (2012), "The Perceived Benefits of Agri-tourism: The Provider's Perspective", *Tourism Management*, 33, pp. 215-224.

Vogt, L. (2014), "The Economic Side of Agri-tourism: Business Performance and Competitive Factors", *Economia agro-alimentare*, pp. 77-102.

World Tourism Organization (WTO) (2001), "Tourism Satellite Accounts: Recommended Methodological Framework", New York, United Nations.

7

Medical Tourism in India: An Emerging Market

Sarba N. Mishra and Nirakar Pattanaik

Introduction

Medical tourism is an emerging concept though it has historical roots. India emerged as the 4th largest tourist destination from the point of view of health and treatment. A liberal and secular country, hospitable people, bonafide physicians and surgeons, less costly medicines, alternate medicines, and caring nurses has attracted patients around the world. In the last few decades, it has been observed that people from Middle East (Gulf countries), Europe and even US are visiting India and taking treatment from the urban hospitals. According to International Medical Journal, "medical tourism is defined as the providing of cost effective medical services in collaboration with the tourism industry for patients needing surgical and other forms of special treatment.

Medical tourism may be a nascent industry but the concept is very old". India is the country of Charak and Susruta of 6th century BC who developed the Ayurveda and the surgeries with scientific explanations. India has infinite possibilities to attract international tourists to provide treatment, by surpassing some of its inherent weaknesses and threats. Various dimensions of medical tourism are discussed in this paper with data and empirical observations to justify it.

India as a Preferred Destination for Medical Tourism

Recent decades have seen a tremendous growth in private sector investment in healthcare. Hospitals established by the private corporate players are of world class. They have not only the latest medical technological facilities but also the services of Indian doctors and nurses with a high degree of proficiency.

Corporate hospitals are completely equipped, up market and proficient and can measure up, or even outshine, any hospital in the West. India is able to offer highly cost competitive medical treatment with the most up-to-date technological advances.

The quality of service coupled with comparatively low charges for common surgeries has made India an attractive destination for medical travel. The Indian Government has moved to provide visa facilities for the medical tourists. The main clientele comes from the SAARC countries but an increasing number of non-resident Indians (NRIs) settled in the US and the UK have also been availing of the healthcare services in India.

There is a good prospect of patients coming from the Middle East in future. The main impediment for medical tourists coming from the UK and US for major surgeries is the fact that the insurance companies are generally not willing to cover treatment in India. However, the cost savings involved in getting treatment done in India is bound to break barriers imposed by the insurance companies. Already some hospitals are entering into alliance with international insurance companies for making it possible to send patients to India for treatment.

The competitiveness of India in medical value travel is enhanced by the attractiveness of the alternative systems of medicine, *Ayurveda* in particular, for the foreign tourists. A large number of tourists, both domestic and foreign, undergo treatment under *Ayurveda* not only for improving their fitness and well-being but also for curing many types of chronic diseases.

For the regulation of *Ayurveda* clinics and for ensuring that they employ techniques in accordance with traditional methods, the Ministry of Health and Family Welfare has issued guidelines to be used by the States. Accordingly, Kerala, the most popular destination for tourists for treatment under *Ayurveda* has promulgated an ordinance regulating *Ayurveda* health centres.

The ordinance requires registration of such centres and prescribes facilities and medical staff that they must have in order to run them. The unique position that Kerala enjoys with respect to *Ayurveda* is due to the fact that the treatment in the State has proved effective in dealing with certain diseases, which are incurable by other systems. The State is also well endowed with herbs and medicinal plants, which are used for treatment.

Objectives and Methodology

The objective of the study is to find out the causes of emergence of the medical tourism which since the 16th century had an impact on the income and development of the host countries. Other countries competing with India and their relative advantages are also studied. Other aspects include weaknesses and threats we face from international markets and various opportunities associated with the medical tourism in India. Moreover, the infrastructure and institutional changes desired to make India the best place for medical tourism are also discussed.

Normally, secondary data is taken and we use the time series analysis to justify it. The hypothesis is that the political and social condition of India will remain conducive and normal for a period of time. The international war and internal conflict are assumed as a rare situation and its impact cannot be discussed.

Medical Tourism Defined

An emerging trend, though seems novice, yet the old concept is the cynosure of the physicians, government, tourism ministry and philanthropists in recent era. Medical tourism is a comprehensive term which is defined by International Medical Journal as follows, "medical tourism is defined as providing of cost-effective medical services in collaboration with the tourism industry for patients needing surgical and other forms of special treatment". Medical tourism refers to the act of travelling to another country to seek specialised or economical medical care, well-being and recuperation of acceptable quality with the help of support system.

According to Dr. Arunprashad, "medical tourism is a phenomenon of people travelling to other countries to obtain medical, dental, and surgical care while at the same time touring, vacationing, and fully experiencing the attractions of the countries that they are visiting. Exorbitant costs of healthcare in industrialized nations, ease and affordability of international travel, favourable currency exchange rates in the global economy, rapidly improving technology and standards of care in many countries of the world, and most importantly proven safety of healthcare in select foreign nations have all led to the rise of medical tourism. More and more people are travelling abroad as an affordable, enjoyable, and safe alternative to having medical, dental, and surgical procedures done in their home countries".

The main determinant of medical tourism is cost of treatment, its accessibility and time period and quality care.

Medical tourism market is estimated to be around US$ 100 billion. More than 25 countries are serving around a million medical tourists annually. The prominent countries are Thailand, Malaysia, Costa Rica, Mexico and India. The other causes can be summarised as follows:

1. **Low Cost:** Low cost of health treatment is one of the major reasons behind medical tourism. Treatment available in lower cost with improved/better services is always preferred by the people. People want minimum investment and maximum benefit out of it.
2. **Medical Facility:** Existing medical facility is also one of the reasons for the growth of medical tourism. Most of the

underdeveloped and developing countries are not having infrastructure for proper medical services.

3. **Expertise:** Lack of expertise in the field of healthcare and treatment is also one of the reasons for medical tourism. Many countries like Saudi Arabia, Middle East and UAE etc. are lacking expertise in medical field despite the infrastructure they have.
4. **National Insurance Policy:** Government insurance scheme or scheme provided by the insurance companies is also one of the reasons for medical tourism across the world. Insurance companies do not cover all the treatments and they vary accordingly. The treatment which is not covered and if it is costly it promotes people to go for some other alternates like treating it somewhere else at a lower cost.
5. **Waiting List:** Long waiting time for the treatment is also one of the reasons for medical tourism. Shortage of both doctors and hospital beds in many countries especially in Europe also contribute to medical tourism. Patients generally do not prefer to be in trouble or in pain for longer period of time rather prefer fast and early treatment from outside.
6. **Ethical Issues:** Ethical issues in medical practices cause increment in medical tourism. Patient care, interpersonal skills, medical knowledge and work in the interest of patient are important aspects of medical treatment and the resultant medical tourism.
7. **Government Policy:** Countries like India, Cuba, Malaysia and Thailand are inviting more investments in medical industry and expediting hassle free approval process. Various offers and promotions are given to the tourists to attract them and by giving them preferences than in regular tourism.
8. **Fashion and Life Style:** Life style and fashion is also one of the important factors behind medical tourism. People in many countries go for life style treatments instead of treatment for

any particular disease. These popular treatments include facelift, tummy tuck and botox treatments.

Government of India is focusing on medical tourism and on health care sector by providing better infrastructure and support to the hospitals. Apart from it, the Ministry of Tourism is also taking various steps for the promotion of medical tourism in India. These measures include:

Medical Visas: Initiative has been taken by the current government for immediate medical visas for SAARC countries' residents.

Swachh Bharat Abhiyan: Swachh Bharat Abhiyan initiative taken by the Prime Minister of India will change the customer perception of an unhygienic country. There has also been participation in world travel trade shows to showcase our presence at the international level.

Marketing Development: Ministry of Tourism has recently revised guidelines for the Marketing Development Assistance Scheme (MDA) for medical tourism. The financial support for marketing will be provided to the approved tourism service providers. The service providers are the representatives of the hospitals. These hospitals have to be accredited by the Joint Commission for International Accredited Hospitals (JCI) and National Accreditation Board of Hospitals (NABH). A medical tourism service provider is referred to as MTSP and wellness tourism service provider is known as WTSP.

Road Shows: Road shows are organized by the Ministry of Tourism from time-to-time to promote the silent and key features of medical tourism in the country. Road shows have been organized in Dubai, Riyadh and Kuwait.

Language: Language is always a barrier for the tourists in the world. There is no language barrier in India as a majority of doctors and nurses are able enough to communicate in English.

Medical Tourism Market Report, 2015

The report found that India is "one of the low cost and

high quality medical tourism destinations and offers a wide variety of procedures at about one-tenth the cost of similar procedures in the United States".

India is unique as a tourist destination due to the following reasons:

- India has the provision of organ donation like kidneys and can save patients from death.
- The provision of surrogacy of mother is legalised which is helpful to get a child.
- Except Malaysia, India is the second country to use herbal medicines to treat patients through a holistic manner with no side effects.
- Alternate courses of treatment like yoga, acupressure, hydrotherapy and other therapies (including naturopathy) are used to treat patients.
- The Indian service industry people are soft and hospitable in nature like Philippines and Sri Lanka which is the reason for increase in medical tourism in India.
- The cost of medicine is the least in India which is advantageous for a medical tourist. Among all the South Asian countries, the medicine cost is the least in India.
- India is a secular and liberal country, so people of any religion will feel at home for taking treatment.
- There is no language barrier like China or Russia, since 75 percent of the population can understand and speak English.
- The Government of India has introduced various steps to reduce the prices of various life saving drugs, which will further make the treatment cost-effective.
- The step taken by Tatas to provide 24 hour help to cancer patients through a telephonic call and by providing insurance health cover to include ayurveda and naturopathy is a facility normally not provided by any country in the world.
- India is a country with natural beauty and weather varies from extreme to moderate which can be conducive for

people from any part of the world.

- The development of information technology, banking and insurance sector will attract many foreign tourists to take treatment in health related issues.

Advantages of medical treatment in India include reduced costs, the availability of latest medical technologies, and a growing compliance on international quality standards. Foreigners are less likely to face a language barrier in India since the doctors and the attached personnel are well trained in English language. Unlike Saudi Arabia, India is a liberal and secular country to deal with people of different religions. Table 7.1 indicates India's rank among the top 14 medical tourist destinations in the world.

Most common treatments include dental care, cosmetic surgery, elective surgery, and fertility treatment. The driving forces behind medical tourism in the country include advanced technology, better quality care, quick access to medically necessary procedures, lower costs of drugs, and affordable rates for discretionary procedures. The increasing trend of patients is a positive indicator and India is expecting US$ 8 billion earnings from medical tourism by 2020.

Table 7.1: Top 14 Medical Tourist Destinations by Volume of Care

Rank	Country	Rank	Country
1.	Thailand	8.	Costa Rica
2.	Hungary	9.	Brazil
3.	India	10.	Mexico
4.	Singapore	11.	South Korea
5.	Malaysia	12.	Columbia
6.	Philippines	13.	Belgium
7.	United States	14.	Turkey

In terms of number of patients, India gets the third highest number of patients for treatment. Thailand and Hungary are getting more patients than India due to weather conditions.

Comparatively, India gets more patients from Bangladesh, Maldives and Afghanistan. All the three countries are economically underdeveloped and neighbouring countries of India (Table 7.2).

Table 7.2: Country-wise Break-up of Medical Tourists in India (2012)

(percent)

Country	Share
USA	2
UAE	2
Russia	3
Oman	3
Sri Lanka	3
Nigeria	6
Iraq	8
Afghanistan	9
Maldives	17
Bangladesh	22
Others	25

The major airports and cities where the tourists arrive in India is depicted in Table 7.3. All the metro cities excluding Kolkata are at the top. The Government of India has given extensive transformation to the airports particularly the IGI airport at Delhi to provide enhanced facilities. World class facilities and security is ensured at the airport with linkage to metro services to make it cost-effective (Table 7.3).

The government has outlined a prominent and important role for medical tourism in India. Traditionally, the healthcare sector of India has struggled to cater to the domestic needs because of the deficit in infrastructure and technical manpower.

However, with the advent of private hospitals and the evolution of industry as a whole, quite a large number of private sector hospitals are now equipped with world class infrastructure and facilities. The role of government led by Prime Minister Narendra Modi in facilitating this trajectory has been monumental.

Table 7.3: Foreign Tourist Arrivals by Port of Entry

(as in 2014)

Point of Entry	Percent Share
Delhi Airport	30.20
Mumbai Airport	19.00
Chennai Airport	8.80
Bengaluru Airport	6.30
Hyderabad Airport	3.10
Kolkata Airport	3.00
Others	29.60

However, we still have a long way to go in developing our medical infrastructure. In comparison to countries like US, Australia and China, the cost of drugs and medical personnel in India is relatively cheap which has been able to generate demand for medical tourism in India.

Table 7.4 indicates that the cost of treatment is least in India. In 2016 alone, approximately more than 2,00,000 tourists arrived on medical visa for their treatment and this number is increasing each year by 40-45 percent.

The medical tourism industry of India in 2015 was estimated at US$ 3 billion and is projected to grow to US$ 7-8 billion by 2020.

Table 7.4: Cost of Treatment

Cost (in US$)

Procedure	United States	Thailand	Singapore	Malaysia	India
Heart bypass	1,30,000	11,000	18,500	9,000	7,000
Heart valve replacement	1,60,000	10,000	12,500	9,000	9,500
Hip replacement	43,000	12,000	12,000	10,000	7,020
Knee replacement	40,000	10,000	13,000	8,000	9,200

Drawbacks

These can be listed as under:

1. Many areas outside of the major cities may be unsettling for foreign visitors who are not accustomed to seeing large scale poverty. This being said, however, both the hospitals and hotels are otherwise totally safe, modern, clean, and have world-class facilities.
2. The current wave of fresh investment in the healthcare delivery segment in India by several big corporate houses has resulted in upgradation of the quality of services provided and improvement in health indicators. Although the basic health indicators have improved, a lot remains to be done in terms of infrastructure.
3. A national master plan must take into account the major problems of manpower training for medical tourism. The success of medical tourism depends upon visitor satisfaction which in turn depends upon good and effective services. Hospitals, travel agencies, tour operators and government tourist offices all require trained staff. There is a need for massive training programme at the sub-regional and regional levels. India produces 45,000 doctors every year but the quality of the doctors in private colleges is not satisfactory, which needs to be addressed.

Suggestions for Revamping Medical Tourism in India

Medical tourism is an international dimension of the growth of the healthcare industry. Thailand has been able to attract more than 1 million medical tourists due to world class infrastructure facilities in Thailand. India should be able to replicate the Thailand example by focusing on development of good quality medical as well as tourism infrastructure. India certainly has the potential and the capacity to attract more than 1 million tourists per annum.

As per the report of WHO, India needs more health workers, doctors and medical professionals. There are 426 MBBS colleges in India including AIIMS and JIPMER with approximately 63,835 medical seats.

Maximum medical and para-medical colleges are in southern States. The quality of education in few private medical colleges may not be up to the mark. Consequently, a strict monitoring by agencies like Medical Council of India (MCI) or Indian Council of Medical Research (ICMR) should be undertaken to ensure the quality of doctors being produced in the country.

The brain drain of top Indian doctors to UK and US also is another cause of low doctor-patient ratio. The government should provide better facilities and remuneration to stop this outflow which would further enhance the medical treatment scenario in the country.

Strengthening the sources of finance and promulgating the investment policy for development of medical tourism can be taken up. Insurance and bank facilities should be upgraded for easier facilitation of foreign tourists arriving in India.

A pragmatic policy framework should be designed which ensures that medical tourism creates employment in the country. Necessary provisions for vocational training facilities for supporting staff and other paramedical staff should be outlined.

Master plan should be devised to promote medical tourism in different cities all over the country which have hitherto not been covered yet.

References

Carrera, P.M. and Bridges, J.F.P (2006), "Globalization and Healthcare: Understanding Health and Medical Tourism", *Expert Review of Pharma Economics and Outcomes Research*, 6(4), pp. 447-454.

Connell, J. (2006), "Medical Tourism: Sea, Sun, Sand and Surgery", *Tourism Management*, 27(6), pp. 1093-1100.

Deo, Madhav G. (2013), "Doctor Population Ratio for India: The Reality", *Indian Journal of Medical Research,* 137(4).

Goodrich, G. and Goodrich, J. (1987), "Healthcare Tourism: An Exploration Study", *Tourism Management*, September, pp. 217-222.

Laws, E. (1996), "Health Tourism: A Business Opportunity Approach", in S. Clift and S.J. Page (eds.), 'Health and the International Tourist' Routledge: London and New York.

Peacock, L. (2009), "Medical Tourism in India", Smart Travel Asia, available at: http://www.smarttravelasia.com/medicaltourism.html.

Prasad, C.B. Venkata Krishna (n.d.), "Medical Tourism Industry: Advantage India", Conference on Global Competition and Competitiveness of Indian Corporate.

8

Role of Social Media in the Promotion of Tourism

Aditya Kumar Tripathi and Rakesh Kumar

Introduction

In the common parlance, the term social media marketing (SMM) refers to the use of different social media platforms such as Facebook, Twitter, YouTube etc. for the purpose of promoting a brand, product or any kind of services provided by a particular company/organization. It is also nowadays used for engaging the customers and creating brand loyalty. India is a country which is well renowned for its cultural diversity and rich historical heritage which simply means that it can be developed as a tourism hub and government has taken various initiatives in order to develop it as a tourist spot.

According to Indian Tourism Statistics at a Glance, 2017, India's rank in international tourist arrivals was 25th and its rank in international tourism receipt was 13th which is quite above than most of the countries and this sector of economy is growing rapidly. The report says that annual tourist arrivals in India was 8.80 million depicting an annual growth rate of 9.7 percent which is much more than the international tourist arrival growth rate of 3.9 percent. India earned ₹ 1,54,146 crore of foreign exchange from the tourism industry which shows an annual growth rate of 14 percent. From the above mentioned statistics, it can be deduced that this sector is growing rapidly and there are huge opportunities that can be exploited with the help of social media use in this industry for promotional purposes.

Social media has impact on our daily lives in this current

digital age and tourism industry cannot be left untouched by this. In 2013, Walt Disney spent US$ 524 million on television ads and US$ 140 on internet advertising whereas Toyota spent US$ 959 million on television ads and US$ 112 million on internet advertising. The above data shows us that a tourism and amusement company spends more on internet ads compared to other industries. A normal individual spends about two hours (approx. 116 minutes) via web-based networking.

YouTube comes in initially, expending more than 45 minutes of a man day. Facebook clients will spend a normal of 35 minutes every day. Snapchat and Instagram come in next with 25 minutes and 15 minutes spent every day. Most of the people nowadays use online websites like Make MyTrip, Trivago etc. to plan and schedule their journeys instead of traditional means for decision-making processes related to travel. Although, the Government of India has identified the use of social media and has started its use as a tool for promotion and attraction of consumers, yet its major portion of expenses in publicity is on television advertising.

Review of Literature

Review of literature is very important and an integral part of any research work in order to get an insight about the various researches already done related to the topic.

Various research papers have been studied relating to the use of social media as a tool for marketing and promoting and also what is their impact on the decision-making process of the present and potential consumers.

In a study done by Sema, 2013, she concluded that the use of social networks in travel planning has a positive impact on the experience derived from the travel and also opined that when people are satisfied, they share their travel experiences. These results show that when the perceived level of enjoyment is high, the usage of social networks increase as a source in travel planning and the level of experience with social networks has a positive influence on the exchange of travel experiences on such networks. Hence, it can be said that the social network platforms and the level of perceived enjoyment are interrelated for greater fun—greater use of social networks for greater travel planning.

Yang, 2012, in his study identified that there is a close relationship between consumer decision-making and the use of social networks, which shows that social networks influence the brand, advertising activities and consumer buying intentions. He also said that it is not necessary to influence the decision-making process of the consumer, but can have an intercession impact.

Social networks can develop brand attitudes that influence buying behaviour. The good image of the brand or product can lead the consumer to make a decision about their purchases. When a consumer in social network shares or recommends services or products, it influences the attitude of the brand and influences its decision-making process. However, advertising on social networks, provided by commercial sources, affects both the attitude of the consumer and the intention to buy. From that information, it helps marketers plan their marketing strategies. Many marketers use social media for marketing campaigns. It is an easy way to communicate with the consumers; also it is inexpensive to advertise brands or services. Social media is not only for advertising, but it can also be a tool for brands or services to connect with their consumers.

Another study shows that social networks allow consumers and potential consumers to communicate directly with a brand representative. Since most consumers use social networks as a tool to find and purchase articles, brands or services, they use this advantage to promote their products. Online purchasing is a booming market all over the world and is giving a global level of intercultural segmentation (Simona Vinerean, 2013). If they have problems with products or services, consumers can communicate with the company through social networks, which is an easy way to connect and get in touch with them. Companies face the challenge of how they chose to react to comments or responses on social networks. One's reactions and responses can generate strong images of the brand and bring more consumers to buy products or services.

When a consumer wants to make a decision on the product, every single detail could be an influence to their decision-making. Consumer motives for engaging in social media provide insights into consumers' activities. Consumers have three main gratifications or motives for using the internet as a medium, namely, information, entertainment, and social aspects (Heinonen, 2011).

Major Social Networking Sites/Platforms for Promotion of Tourism Industry

Facebook: It is an American social networking service provider company based in Menlo Park, California. It was launched on February 4, 2004 by Mark Zuckerberg. This social networking site has the most number of active users numbering about 2.2 billion. It is estimated that around 10 lakh small and medium-sized businesses use this site to promote their businesses; hence is an important tool of digital marketing. India, Brazil and Indonesia have the largest target audience after the US. Therefore, with growing audiences of Facebook, one cannot ignore the use of social media in tourism industry in order to attract tourists and create a brand image.

Twitter: Twitter was established on March 21, 2006 by Jack Dorsey and is based in San Francisco, California. Most of the organizations use this platform for getting real time feedbacks and providing information by ways of tweets/retweets. Targeted ads with specific audiences is one of the basic features of this site.

YouTube: This social media platform was founded by three PayPal employees on February 14, 2005. It is nowadays owned by Google and is the second most popular search engine after Google. This platform is used by many digital marketers for advertising. It is considerably much cheaper and can target much more audiences as being the second most popular search engine-cum-networking site.

Instagram: It was launched on October 6, 2010 and is owned and managed by Facebook. There are more than 400 million users which are active on this platform who share information related to travel, fashion, food, art and related areas. This site has the most potential for being used as a tourism industry promotional tool.

LinkedIn: This professional networking can be used for generating B2B contacts and businesses. It also helps a business in getting new business and can also be used for attracting new and more competitive professionals.

From the above, it can be interpreted that 94 percent of the social media marketers use Facebook ads as a tool of advertising their brands and products followed by Instagram which is used by 24 percent of the marketers and then LinkedIn and Twitter follow the series of major choices by 16 percent and 15 percent respectively. These statistics prove that most of the brands and businesses prefer different social media platforms for advertising their products/brands in which Facebook is the major platform of all. Use of social media platforms in tourism industry can be much more economical and can target a large number of audiences to engage with the places they would like to visit and can also create increased business for the tourism sector. This can be done by either paid form of social media advertising or with the help of viral marketing concept.

Role of Social Media in Promoting Tourism Industry

Effective Promotional Programme: The social media platforms give an opportunity to the marketers to make their promotional programmes much more effectively. It is the tendency of the consumers that they are much more loyal towards those brands which treat them as their most important assets and do not avoid customers once the sales is done.

Social media sites such as Twitter, Facebook, Instagram etc. provide a platform through which it can connect with the customers and can treat them more effectively.

Social media can play a very important role in tourism industry for spreading awareness about the places which one can visit and also gives chance to business houses to remind the users constantly at a very low cost.

Tool for Tourist Service and Feedback: Nowadays, every one of us uses social media for sharing the travel experiences, asking for feedback, and engaging with the brands. Social media platforms have also emerged as a tool for providing services to its customers in no time. They just tweet and share and their problem is solved. This is all possible due to the social media whereby a customer can now directly engage with the brands and the problem is solved in no time. This feature of social media can be exploited by the companies engaged in tourism business also. It lets the companies know about the perception of customers about their brands and to act accordingly.

Communication and Branding: Communication is one of the most important factors that can lead to the success of any organization and helps in creating goodwill. With the help of social media, one can easily interact with its present and future customers and this process of communicating with its customers can lead to branding and creating goodwill in the eyes of the customers because they feel they are valuable for the company and long-term relationship can be thus developed. Social media platforms can be used by the tourist agencies for communicating with their customers and can create a long lasting brand image.

Online Presence of Business Can Generate More Customers: Social media is one of the most important parts of our lives, as an average individual daily spends nearly 2 hours on social media platforms. So, it is more likely that our decision-making process is influenced by the content on these platforms. From sharing of details about dinner to complaining about bad services, individuals share/discuss nearly everything about their lives on these platforms. Hence, tourism industry needs to increase their online presence; brands which have online presence are found to be more authentic by the customers than those who do not have any kind of online presence.

Conclusion

From this paper, it can be concluded that social media platforms play an important role in marketing and promotional activities. The time spent by the users on an average on the social media is growing rapidly and it will have a major impact on the consumer's decisions-making process. Therefore, it has become important for every marketer to develop an online marketing program in order to attract more number of customers and retain the existing ones. Effective use of social media can help in gaining a competitive advantage and if one ignores the use of this tool, can be left behind.

Tourism industry is one of the fastest growing industries in the economy and has potential to generate more output if properly promoted and developed and use of social media can play a very important role in promoting this industry at a very low cost. Government and other agencies involved in this sector should use these sites as a promotional tool for creating and attracting more business for the sector.

References

Asano, E. (2017), "Social Media Today", available at: https://www.socialmediatoday.com/marketing/how-much-time-do-people-spend-social-media-infographic.

Heinonen, K. (2011), "Consumer Activity in Social Media: Managerial Approaches to Consumers' Social Media Behavior", *Journal of Consumer Behaviour*, pp. 356-364.

Jashi, C. (2013), "Significance of Social Media Marketing in Tourism", 8th Silk Road International Conference on Development of Tourism in Black and Caspian Seas Regions.

Mania, A. (2017), "Small Business Trends", available at: https://smallbiztrends.com/2016/05/popular-social-media.

Sema, P. (2013), "Does Social Media Affect Consumer Decsionmaking?", MBA Student Scholarship, Paper 29.

Simona Vinerean, I.C. (2013), "The Effects of Social Media Marketing on Online Consumer Behavior", *International Journal of Business and Management*, 66.

Wicks, D. (2015), "Social Media Today", available at: https://www.socialmediatoday.com/social-business/role-social-media-marketing-business.

Yang, T. (2012), "The Decison Behaviour of Facebook Users", *Journal of Computer Information Systems,* 52(3), pp. 50-59.

9

Electronic Tourism (E-tourism) and Sustainable Development

Veenu Mehra

Introduction

Tourism is a collection of activities, services and industries. It delivers a travel experience comprising transportation, accommodation, eating and drinking establishments, retail shops, entertainment business and the hospitality services. It provides for individual or group travelling away from home. The sum of the phenomena and relationships arising from the interaction of tourists, business suppliers, host governments and host communities in the process of attracting these tourists and other visitors fall on tourism.

It is a fact that influence of growing internet on customer behaviours will manage emerging marketing processes. E-tourism develops searching engines, the transport capacities and the speed of the networks. It influences the number of tourists from all over the world. It uses technology for planning and documenting their journeys. E-tourism offers a possibility to identify the customers and to buy products. It provides support for the global tourism industry. It offers efficient instruments for tourism agents. It develops and distributes their offer globally. The technology favours the future developments in the tourism industry. E-Tourism is a system of establishing commercial relationships of tourism products like flights, hotel reservations, car rentals etc.

What is E-Tourism?

E-tourism includes any communication device or

application, encompassing radio, television, cellular phones, computer hardware and software, satellite systems and the various services and applications associated with them. It includes video conferencing and distance learning. E-tourism reflects the digitisation of all processes and value chains in the tourism, travel, hospitality and catering industries. It includes e-commerce and applies ICTs for maximising the efficiency and effectiveness of the tourism organisation. E-tourism revolutionises all business processes, the entire value chain as well as the strategic relationships of tourism organisations with all their stakeholders. E-tourism increasingly determines the competitiveness of the organisation. It is important for the competitiveness of the industry in the long run.

The concept of e-tourism includes all business functions (i.e. e-commerce, e-marketing, e-finance and e-accounting, e-HRM, e-R&D, e-production) and e-strategy, e-planning and e-management for all sectors of the tourism industry. It includes tourism, travel, transport, leisure, hospitality, intermediaries and public sector organisations.

E-commerce and E-business

E-commerce is the process of buying, selling, or exchanging products, services, or information via computer networks, including the internet. The terms are used interchangeably. E-business includes not only purchasing and selling but also includes servicing the customers and working together with the business associates. It also includes conducting electronic learning and performing e-transactions both internally and externally by an organisation.

E-intervention

An electronic intervention controls information flow in cyberspace for marketing. The most well-known e-intervention in the tourism industry is Trip Advisor and Holiday Check. Its implementation through a Web 2.0 approach, integrates the users as producers of a trusted content.

E-tourism Stakeholders

The main stakeholders in the tourism industry include governments, tour operators, hotels, airlines and other transport operators, and tourists or consumers. These holders have a stake in the development of the electronic market. Each is expected to be affected in different ways by the changes through electronic commerce.

The concerns and interests of these stakeholders need to be addressed in order to ensure that changes are managed and promoted to the benefit of all. Each one of them utilises information and communication technology in their processes to complement each other on making e-tourism efficient. Some of the e-tourism activities performed by the main stakeholders are discussed below.

E-airlines: Earlier, bookings and reservations by airlines were made on physical display boards, where the travellers were listed. Travel agencies had to locate the finest routes and fares in physical form and then check availability and make bookings by phone, prior to issuing a ticket manually.

Distribution is a vital component of airlines' approach and competitiveness. It determines the cost and the capacity to access the travellers. The cost of distribution is increasing considerably and airlines find it difficult to control. The communication technology is now being used heavily to support the distribution of airline seats. This has forced all the players in the aviation industry to recognise the need for re-engineering the distribution processes, costs and pricing structures. Airlines are now focusing on the following aspects:

- Improving the accessibility for customers and their business associates.
- Electronic bookings.
- Online ticketing.
- Yield management.
- E-auctions for very last minute available seats.
- Disintermediation and restructuring of agency charge schemes.

- Increasing the productivity of the new channel in electronic distribution.

E-hospitality: E-hospitality offers support and services to the visitors. It counsels through the phone system and voice mail to pay per view (PPV) movies, secure high speed in rooms, lobby kiosks, and even guest printing/faxing from the guest rooms. Hotels use information and communication technology to improve their operations, manage their inventory and maximise their profitability. Their systems facilitate both in-house management and distribution through electronic media. Property management systems (PMSs) coordinate front office, sales, planning and operational functions by administrating reservations and managing the hotel inventory. PMSs integrate the "back" and "front" of the house management and improve general administration functions. It includes accounting and finance; marketing research and planning; forecasting and yield management; payroll and personnel; and purchasing. Hotel chains gain more benefits from PMSs, as they can introduce a unified system for planning, budgeting and controlling and coordinating their properties centrally.

E-tour Operators: Leisure travellers often purchase "packages", consisting of charter flights and accommodation, arranged by the tour operators. Tour operators tend to pre-book these products and distribute them through brochures displayed in travel agencies. The tour operators realised the benefits of utilising communication technology in organising, promoting, distributing and coordinating their packages. They developed databases and established electronic links with the travel agencies. The aim of tour operators is to reduce their information handling costs and increase the speed of information transfer and retrieval. This has certainly improved their productivity and capacity management.

E-travel Agencies: E-tourism has become a major tool for travel agencies. They provide information and reservation facilities and support the midway between consumers and providers. It includes various reservation systems, which mainly enable them to check availability and make reservations for tourism products. Global distribution system (GDS) have been critical for travel agencies to access information and make reservations on scheduled airlines, hotel chains, car rentals services etc. GDSs help to provide up to-date schedules, prices and availability information, as well as an effective reservation method. They offer internal management modules integrating the back office including accounting, commission monitor, personnel and front office covering customers' history, itinerary construction, ticketing and communication with suppliers.

E-purposes: The planning, management and coordination functions of destinations have been undertaken by either the public sector or by partnerships between stakeholders of the local tourism industry. E-purposes are never considered a critical instrument for the development and management of destinations increasingly. E-purpose facilitates the tourist experience before, during and after the visit and by coordinating all partners involved in the production and delivery of tourism. E-purpose utilises communication technology to promote tourism policy and coordinate the operational functions.

Vision of E-tourism

The development of e-tourism has made significant impacts on the operation, structure and strategy of organisations and their communication with consumers. This has improved the reliability, compatibility and inter-connectivity of numerous terminals and applications. Therefore, the vision of e-tourism can be understood by the following parameters.

For Sponsors:

- Locating customers and/or suppliers worldwide, at a reasonable cost.
- Reduction in cost of information processing, storage, and

distribution.

- Reduced delays, inventories, and cost through supply chain improvements.
- Customization/personalization at a reasonable cost.
- Facilitation in innovation and enabling of unique business models.
- Lower communication cost.
- Saving of time and reduction in cost by enabling e-procurement.
- Improvement in customer service and relationship through direct interactions with customers.
- Minimization of customized inventories.
- Reduction in distribution costs by delivering online benefits to consumers.

For Stakeholders:

- Shopping any time from any place because of ubiquity.
- Enhanced selection to choose from a variety of channels.
- Customization of products and/or services.
- Comparative rates.
- Digitized products that can be downloaded immediately upon payment.

Challenges of E-tourism

E-tourism is understood as a mechanism to improve the quality of life of local people. It depends upon systematic control and management with respect to its visionary goals. However, it requires crucial efforts to remove the challenges in the path of management of this process. The challenges are summarised below:

- Lack of universal standards for quality, security, and reliability.
- Insufficient bandwidth of telecommunications.
- Evolving software development tools.
- Integrating internet and e-commerce software with existing applications and databases.

- Security and privacy concerns which deter customers from buying.
- Lack of trust in e-commerce and in unknown sellers which hinders buying.
- People do not yet sufficiently trust paperless and faceless transactions.
- Many legal and public policy issues, including taxation, have not yet been resolved or are not clear.
- National and international government regulations sometimes get in the way.
- Sellers and buyers that are needed for profitable e-commerce operations are insufficient.
- Monitoring of online fraud.

Sustainable E-tourism

The tourism industry has responded to these challenges by applying the concept of sustainable development to tourism policy and planning i.e. sustainable tourism development. This sustainable tourism development can become an effective concept in goal management through e-tourism. It is a positive, comprehensive and integrated approach to tourism development. It involves resource management and working together with stakeholders for the long-term viability and quality of the social, economic and environmental resources. They develop goals in a sustainable fashion by using various indicators including monitoring, eco-labelling, codes of conduct, educating tourists and other best practices. These approaches should be documented as having quality, technical content, reliability, maturity, equity and effectiveness. The existing difficulties in the current approaches and tools in congruence to harmonious growth can become an effective step towards sustainability.

Conclusion

Future of e-tourism is focused on consumer-centric technologies. Networking has become dynamic. It associates partnership with consumers. It works proactively and reactively.

It supports organizations to interact with their customers. The development of new and powerful e-tourism applications empowers suppliers and the stakeholders. It enhances their efficiency and re-engineers their communication strategies. E-tourism develops their own basis of knowledge and improves the management and marketing functions.

References

Ali, A. and Frew, A.J. (2010), "ICT and its Role in Sustainable Tourism Development", *Information and Communication Technologies in Tourism*, pp. 479-491, available at: https://link.springer.com/chapter/10.1007/978-3-211-99407-8_40.

Cooper, C. (ed.), "Contemporary Tourism Reviews", Oxford: Goodfellow Publishers.

Condratov, I. (2013), "E-tourism: Concept and Evolution", *Ecofourm Journal*, 2(12), pp. 58-61, available at: http://www.tugberkugurlu.com/archive/definintion-of-tourism-unwto-definition-of-tourism-what-is-tourism.

10

Sustainable Tourism: A Pedagogical Approach

Biswajit Behera

Introduction

Tourism is a social, cultural and economic phenomena related to development. It has a great impact towards economy, natural and artificial environment and above all the local population at the sites visited. Due to this wide range of impacts, more stakeholders are involved. Hence, there is a need for f holistic approach towards tourism development, management and monitoring. This approach is termed as sustainable tourism education.

Sustainable tourism is what meets the needs and demands of present tourists and enhances the opportunity for the future (UNWTO, 2013). It directs the management of all resources in such a way that economic, social, ethical and aesthetic needs can be fulfilled. In that context, essential ecological balance, biological diversity and life systems of local people should be maintained and balanced. Equality of opportunity should be focused in order to ensure equity. The important principle of sustainable development comprising of social, environmental and economic aspects should be embedded with development. UNWTO supports and promotes mainstreaming of tourism in global, national and regional agendas. The key policies are implemented to tackle unemployment, regional development, poverty alleviation and marching towards sustainability.

Issues of Sustainable Tourism

Tourism development should be socially sustainable. The

local level issues of tourism should be resolved. Some social issues that affect societal development must be legislatively cracked. The need and demand of tourism must satisfy with the policy and framework of government in order to solve empowerment. Thus, tourism development faces a number of issues and challenges for its sustainability. What are the most important issues of sustainability?

These are issues of setting goals, sharing of information and public participation, productivity, development of sustainable culture, need and demand of driven factors, attitude, values and behavioural pattern of individuals, use of technology, development of ideas and knowledge creation, impact of demographic changes, needs of individuals, managing equity, and the role of policy and legislation at all levels of government.

Sustainable Tourism Pedagogy

Sustainable tourism pedagogy is a kind of approach to make development of tourism permanent. It will have an impact on the growth of community too. It is linked to the following parameters given in a planned form.

1. Employment: To raise the economic level of local community.
2. Citizenship: To preserve the culture and heritage of the country.
3. Nationality: To feel a sense of belongingness.
4. Environment: To further measures for the protection of environment.
5. Tourism sites/visits: To find tourism products, destinations and modes of transport.
6. Quality: In relation to awareness, relevance, credibility, accuracy and accessibility.

- **Awareness:** The elements include human, financial and technical resources for implementation of tourism education.
- **Relevance:** It reflects the degree to which the programme

of education meets visitor's needs.

- **Credibility**: It refers to the confidence level as to the extent of it being professional.
- **Accuracy:** The information and knowledge is correctly estimated.
- **Accessibility:** Suitability of dissemination through which information can be accessed.

Objectives of Sustainable Tourism Pedagogy

Pedagogy initiates to establish a network of national and international tourism educators. Its purpose is to bring a fundamental change in tourism education from vocational point of view. The strategy is based on five key value areas to be integrated in the tourism curricula:

- Ethics.
- Stewardship.
- Knowledge.
- Professionalism.
- Mutual sharing.

The emphasis is to include the insights and guidance in teaching and learning practices. The vocational work must be blended with higher order 'knowledge' and 'reflective skills' in the practice of teaching sustainable tourism.

Looking at Pedagogy: Sustainability requires interactive experience and engagement with the environmental, economic, social and cultural issues at the local community site. It demands development of multiple literacy. Different types of knowledge (implicit and explicit) are integrated. Sustainable tourism literacy should be identified and explored based on sustainable tourism principles through collaborative approach.

Technical Literacy: This includes foundational technical knowledge related to sustainable development of tourism, inclusive of planning, management and other strategies.

Ecological Literacy: This involves awareness of the linkage between people and their environment, and consequences of decisions and actions upon their relationships etc. to build a natural environment.

Analytical Literacy: This includes skills, techniques and personal capability necessary to engage in problem solving, issue identification, critical thinking ability to examine and evaluate values related to various conversations, discussions, and dialogues on sustainable development.

Multi-cultural Literacy: It includes appreciation of different cultures, values, interests and power relations. Ethnic groups marginalized groups which are discriminated due to gender and other reasons should be considered.

Policy Literacy: This includes knowledge of different policies and frameworks related to tourism development.

Imperatives of Pedagogy

Tourism can surely contribute to sustainable development. It influences an individual's overall life satisfaction. The quality of life depends on components of needs, including basic needs, security needs (like a stable place to live and work), belonging needs (to support social networks and opportunities for participating in social, cultural and political activities) and finally self-esteem needs (to include knowledge and confidence and the ability and freedom to make choices). The desirable factors affecting the quality of life are as under:

- Taking more positive action to improve returns in terms of economy.
- Enhancing working conditions for individuals.
- Improving the environmental performance.
- Improving education.
- Improving managing and learning practice.

Thus, it pertains to rigorous tourism education; more inclusive for all groups of potential tourists and recognition of tourism concerns to embrace technology and to develop strategic plans.

Corporate Social Responsibility (CSR): A specific application of the notion of environment and social auditing towards business practice is related to social responsibility. It is relevant towards sustainable education.

Collaborative Learning: It is an important dimension which addresses critically the sustainability issues. Community participation in decisions involving public goods, cultural sites, and cultural heritage are utmost important. Planning and policy making are participatory actions in a collaborative learning. It results in knowledge building and skill development. Community service learning is democratic in nature. It is a progressive education. It facilitates participation democracy and community building.

Realization of the Potential: It develops a challenge for industry and communities to provide a regular participatory tourism experience which will generate jobs and promote economic development. It can be considered through the following actions.

- Better planning and management—cultural heritage tourism strategies and plans should be linked with the community.
- Coordination at both policy and action levels, among different levels of government involved in tourism development.
- Cooperation among local sites with respect to transportation and minimum facilities.
- Assessment and monitoring-impact assessment including physical, natural, social and cultural limits.
- Comprehensive education and training programmes at the local, regional and national level. This should provide a range of educational services to communities. It can be done through distance education; self-paced computer based learning packages, and publications and manuals oriented for community participants.

Entrepreneurship: Entrepreneurship towards sustainable tourism is a process to create wealth for oneself and to add value to the society. It develops practices of research, site development, planning, preservation of technology and visitors' services. Entrepreneurship is viable in the following areas:

- Community tourism planning.
- Heritage and cultural development.
- Technology.
- Site management.
- Enlightened community involvement.
- Understanding collaborative approaches.

Towards Future Life: Its approach should be based on access to five different types of capital. These include the following.

- Social capital: Quality of relationship and network with other people in the community, opportunities to participate in decision-making and the level of trust within the groups.
- Human capital: It includes personal skills and knowledge as well as educational achievements and opportunities.
- Physical capital: Infrastructure and facilities available for individual and social groups to use.
- Financial capital: Related to income and savings.
- Natural capital: Quality of natural environment and eco-system.

Empowering Indigenous People: The new integrated STP aims to alleviate the problems related to environment like deforestation, erosion and loss of bio-diversity and poverty of many indigenous groups by helping communities to manage their lands sustainably. This pedagogy will help them to manage conservation areas and generate sustainable foresting, and production of handicrafts, organic and other traditional products.

Skill Development: The development of skilled workforce would benefit from the job opportunities that can be generated through tourism. It raises the efficiency level and service through improvement of education and training. Skill development enhances the developmental processes through poverty alleviation and job creation.

Tourism Education: A good practice for vocational education is to link effectively education and training on one hand and industry and employers on the other, so that each one can benefit from other's experience.

Integrated Curriculum

Sustainable pedagogy on tourism considers implementation of core curriculum. Different subjects are included in order to make it multi-disciplinary. The areas like historical development of tourism, tourism statistics, tours and agencies, marketing in tourism, planning and development, organization and finance, future of tourism etc. are some of major subjects of sustainable tourism. The multiple topics that can be included in the curriculum are listed below:

- Career opportunities.
- Industry growth.
- Management skills.
- Vocational skills.
- Opportunities of tourism.
- Education and understanding.
- Needs of tourism industry.
- Decision-making.
- Professionalism.
- Quality.
- Service delivery.
- Competency of tourism analysis and etc.

Process of Learning

The process of pedagogy towards sustainable tourism should signify the cultural heritage and human resource development. It should be as under:

- Integrating living and culture-historical monuments, traditional vernacular villages, rural temples, natural environments which are of particular interest to the visitors. These should form part of cultural landscape of a site.
- Investment in training and human resource development in traditional arts for better tourist economics.
- Thorough training about cultural sites and their

maintenance should be propagated. It is crucial for tourism business.

- Country's cultural and natural resources towards development of tourism industry should be used. It plays an important part towards national economic growth.
- Development towards conservation of the country's cultural and natural heritage should be advocated to find linkage between culture and the environment.
- Community participation in planning of tourism development and implementation of social activities focused on cultural heritage.

Learning Context

It includes vocational and technical knowledge. It involves the social and ethical aspects and engages in critical thinking. The aspects of critical thinking include evolving a problem and negotiating for its solutions.

How the problem is defined, who is involved, understanding the diversity of stakeholders, needs, interests and values are considered. STP integrates theoretical knowledge from a wide range of fields to encourage vocational competence balanced with ethical competence.

Product of Learning

The community members of learning should be self-actualizing reflective individuals. There should be a move from self-oriented system of education to a progressive learner who is oriented towards social action and experiences in the cultural world. It will develop problem solving power, critical thinking skills and overall practical knowledge of the learners. This should be an experiential educational perspective.

It enables a reflective practice, learning to critically examine 'self' in relation to 'others' through engagement with the community. Thus, it needs participatory engagement. It will orient to solve immediate challenges and issues of sustainability. It is a change-oriented pedagogy. It must tackle environmental and social issues. It provides the experience and skills to engage critically with the diversity, gender, minority and related issues of sustainable tourism. Sustainable development has an imperative towards climate change, environmental presentation and cultural conservation. It also impacts human development.

Research Orientation

Researchers define sustainable development of tourism from different angles like environmental protection, social changes, economic activity, environmental balance and improving the living standards of the locals. Indispensable components such as conservation and rehabilitation and local economic development should be integrated with STP. Effective planning and management are the two main aspects towards sustainable development.

Cultural heritage is a main resource to bring about development. Tourism is related to historical buildings, art works, beautiful scenery and other similar aspects. It is also a motivation for utilizing vacations. Cultural attractions include museums, galleries, festivals, local architecture, heritage sites, artistic performances and all attractions related to cuisine, attire, learning and religion.

Planning and management related to how to attract visitors is vital. It consists of design, improvement, capacity, operation and selling of goods as well as services encompassing cultural heritage components. Therefore, the research includes:

- Local people.
- Cultural inheritance.
- Resource protection.
- Tourism planning.
- Tourism management.
- Tourism marketing.
- Talent training.

Thus, research on sustainable development of tourism would entail the following (Figure 10.1):

Figure 10.1: Areas of Research on Sustainable Tourism

Conclusion

The sustainability in the line of Saddler's (1988) consideration of environment, economics and society are incorporated to develop sustainable tourism pedagogy. The indicators of pedagogy and its related assessment are important to practice education and training. This article recommends a guiding prototype to set directions for research. What to approach and how to practice these issues of sustainability in the line of different components of pedagogy are suggested. Starting with core values of quality of life and conservation of nature, the pedagogy gives ample scope for investigations.

References

Bramwell, B. and Lave, B. (1993), "Interpretation and Sustainable Tourism: The Potential and the Pitfalls", *Journal of Sustainable Tourism*, 1(2), pp. 71-80.

Butler, R. (1998), "Sustainable Tourism: Looking Backwards in Order to Progress", in C. Hall and A. Lew (eds.), 'Sustainable Tourism: A Geographical Perspective', Longman, London.

Garrod, B and Fyall, A. (1998), "Beyond the Rhetoric of Sustainable Tourism", *Tourism Management*, 19(3), pp. 199-212.

Hunter, C. and Green, H. (1995), "Tourism and the Environment: A

Sustainable Relationship", Routledge, London.

Liu, Z. (2003), "Sustainable Tourism Development: A Critique", *Journal of Sustainable Tourism*, 11(6), pp. 459-475.

Prosser, R. (1994), "Societal Change and Growth in Alternative Tourism", in E. Cater and G. Lowman (eds.), 'Ecotourism: A Sustainable Option", John Wiley and Sons Inc., New Jersey.

World Tourism Organization (2013), "UNWTO Tourism Highlights", World Tourism Organization, Madrid.

11

Tourism in Jammu and Kashmir: Economic and Environmental Consequences

Naseer Ahmad and Puneeta Pandey

Introduction

Tourism is travel for recreational (fun), leisure (rest), family or business purposes, usually for a limited duration or period. It is commonly associated with international travel, but may also refer to travel to different places within the country. It is a temporary, short-term movement of people to the destination outside their locality (home). According to World Tourism Organization (WTO), tourists are the people "travelling to and staying in places outside their usual environment for not more than one consecutive year for leisure, business and other purposes". Tourism is regarded as one of the major contributing factors of socio-economic development worldwide. Currently, tourism has turned out to be a big commercial sector and has been acknowledged as one of the fastest growing industries.

Tourism sector is principally a service industry because it extends services to various classes of people. Tourism contributes about 9 percent to global gross domestic product (GDP) and also generates 8.7 percent of total jobs. Tourism can play a substantial role in integrating the nations worldwide. Tourism opens up new ways for resources, both investments and generation, leading to employment generation as well as socio-economic development at a large scale. With the promotion and development of technology, accessibility and mobility from one place to another has become quite easier and fast; which is recognized as a positive sign for tourism growth and development. Tourism industry has important socio-economic, environmental and cultural effects, both positive and negative.

Tourism can be a key tool for economic development but it can have serious and destructive consequences on flora and fauna of both terrestrial and aquatic ecosystems, if not properly planned, which in turn results in exploitation of natural resources such as freshwater, forests and marine life.

Tourism industry absolutely affects the environment. Tourism has several harmful effects on various aspects of environment such as air, water, soil, forests, wild life, marine life etc. Uncontrolled conventional tourism causes potential threats to many ecosystems worldwide and lead to serious implications such as soil erosion, increased pollution, dumping and discharge into the seas, loss of natural habitat, increased pressure on endangered species and forest fire vulnerability.

The alteration of the environment at any target tourist destination causes stress in the vicinity. The clearing of existing vegetation or levelling of the terrain for the construction or expansion of roads, parking lots, airport, and hotels has a major disturbing impact on the environment. Other factors such as waste generation, garbage dumping, littering and sewerage may also aggravate the problem.

In the year 2002, the Government of India announced a new tourism policy as an initiative to promote tourism industry. The policy is built around the following 7-S mantras.

1. Swaagat (Welcome).
2. Suchanaa (Information).
3. Suvidhaa (Facilitation).
4. Suraksha (Security).
5. Sahyog (Cooperation).
6. Sanrachnaa (Infrastructure).
7. Safaai (Cleanliness).

Review Literature

Sunlu, 2003, revealed that there is a complex relationship

between tourism and environment. The environmental impacts are caused due to activities like construction of airports, roads, hotels, restaurants, resorts, shopping malls and other tourism related facilities. Tourism has caused severe damage to natural resources, physical environment and the quality of environment. It was suggested that by raising awareness about the environmental values, the natural landscapes can be protected along with the increase in economic importance.

Malik et al., 2013, studied the possible impacts of tourism on environmental conditions in Jammu and Kashmir. In the mountainous region, the tourism related problems include sedimentation and emission from different activities, sewage pollution, soil erosion, landslide, habitat destruction, etc. Tourism related activities pose serious consequences on the environment which include over exploitation of natural resources, loss of habitat and wild life, loss of biodiversity, pollution and waste generation, social and cultural loads to conservation and sustainable use of biodiversity, etc.

Mir, 2014, studied the impact of tourism industry on the economy of Jammu and Kashmir and it was revealed that tourism being an essential tool of economic growth, contributes about 15 percent to state gross domestic product (SGDP). Almost 50-60 percent of the population is directly or indirectly linked with tourism related activities but still some concrete steps should be adopted to facilitate the further development and growth of economy of the state.

Sharma and Raina, 2014, studied the environmental impacts of tourism in Katra town of J&K which constitutes an important place of tourism for the Hindu community. Thousands of pilgrims visit throughout the year, the shrine of Mata Vaishno Devi which is a major contributor towards the growth and development of Katra town. Despite being a largest and fastest growing sector in the global economy, tourism has both positive and negative environmental, social, cultural and economic impacts. But unplanned and unregulated tourism could lead to serious consequences for natural environment. The construction of general infrastructure such as hotels, resorts, etc. for tourism and other commercial purposes pose a serious threat to natural resources which ultimately causes ill-effects on humans and other living organisms. The study also suggested some measures to avoid further deterioration of the natural environment.

From the study of Singh and Unjum, 2016, it was found that tourism plays an important role in the growth of income, employment generation, foreign exchange, etc. Tourism contributed around 7 percent on an average towards the J&K state income during the period. The efforts were made to establish bi-directional relationship between the economic growth and tourism in the state. And with an intention to promote tourism towards new heights of development, there is a need to take some positive steps so that it could be exploited in a much better way and subsequently contributes more comprehensively towards the state's economic growth.

Methodology

The present study is based on secondary information collected from journals, books and other available sources. The paper highlights the growth of economy due to tourism and subsequently the consequences on environmental conditions of Jammu and Kashmir. The possible adverse impacts on the environment include: overexploitation of natural resources, habitat loss of wild life, loss of biodiversity, and pollution in all spheres of ecosystem.

Tourism in Jammu and Kashmir

Jammu and Kashmir is the northern most state of India with Srinagar as the summer capital and Jammu as the winter capital. The state consists of three regions—Jammu, Kashmir valley and Ladakh. The climate of the state differs from sub-tropical in Jammu plains to semi-arctic cold in Ladakh with mountainous tracks in Kashmir having temperate climatic conditions. A large part of the state forms part of the

Himalayan mountains. Thc total geographical area of the state is 2,22,236 square kilometres. The forest ecology comprises of sub-tropical dry deciduous forests, sub-tropical pine forests in Jammu, Himalayan moist temperate forests, Himalayan dry temperate forests; alpine forests in Kashmir and forests in cold arid zone of Ladakh region. The key industries of the state include horticulture, floriculture, handlooms and handicrafts, tourism, mineral-based industry, sericulture, IT and pharmaceuticals.

The state shares its borders with Himachal Pradesh and Punjab, and the neighbouring countries of Pakistan, China and Afghanistan. In the seventeenth century, the Mughal Emperor Jahangir opined,

Gar firdaus bar ruye zamin ast, hamin asto, hamin asto, hamin ast

which means "if there is ever a heaven on earth, it's here, it's here, it's here". Jammu and Kashmir is an important tourist destination and has been a place of attraction for tourists since centuries. The lush green forests, perennial rivers, sweet springs, picturesque alpine scenery and pleasant climate of Kashmir valley, has remained an internationally commendable tourist destination.

The most important tourist destinations include Dal Lake, Mughal Gardens, Gulmarg, Sonamarg, Amarnath shrine, Pahalgam, Shri Mata Vaishno Devi Shrine, Nubra valley, and Pangong Lake.

The state is principally an agrarian state where agriculture occupies an important place in the state economy. On the other hand, nearly 70 percent of the population in the state derives its livelihood directly or indirectly from the agricultural sector. Agriculture is the main contributor of the state's economy. The major crops grown in the state are rice, maize and wheat.

The state of Jammu and Kashmir with its huge potential and growing economy has immense potential for the progression of the tourism industry. Historically, tourism has remained an important tool of growth of economy in the state and has shared a lot in developing the economy, predominantly in Kashmir Valley and Ladakh. This sector has facilitated jobs to a large number of people and generated economic activities chiefly in the tertiary sectors. A clear visible growth is seen in service industry sectors of the state such as transport, hospitality, horticulture and small-scale industries due to tourism development.

The label of tourism has always placed the State of J&K in the fame at the national level as well as the international level. Besides, two Directorates of Tourism for both the regions Jammu and Kashmir, 19 Tourism Development Authorities (TDAs) for main tourist spots, J&K Tourism Development Corporation (JKTDC), Sher-i-Kashmir International Convention Centre (SKICC), J&K State Cable Car Corporation (JKCCC) and Royal Springs Golf Course, Srinagar are operating and functioning for the endorsement and promotion of the tourism sector in the State.

The Directorate of Tourism, Kashmir assess the tourism activities in Kashmir Valley and Ladakh region and also regulates the tourist inflow and coordinates with the other related departments. The directorate is often more engaged in publicity and marketing of the tourism potential of the State at national as well as international level. The Directorate of Tourism, Jammu looks after the tourism of Jammu region and chiefly regulates the pilgrim tourism arrivals in the region. JKTDC undertakes commercial activities like construction of accommodation facilities, running of restaurants, cafeterias and organization of food festivals, and tours and travel activities in and outside the State.

Key Sectors in the State

- Handicrafts have been receiving a priority interest from the government in light of its large employment base and export potential.
- Food processing and agro-based industries prosper in the state due to suitable climate for floriculture and horticulture.

- J&K SIDCO is the nodal agency for development and promotion of medium- and large-scale industries in the state.
- The state is well-known for its small-scale and cottage industries such as pottery, carpet weaving, silks, shawls, basketry, copper and silverware, paper-mache and walnut wood.
- To boost infrastructure, the state has approved funding of about US$ 1.8 billion. Additionally, US$ 120.07 million was earmarked under the Pradhan Mantri Gram Sadak Yojana for the period 2015-16.

Strengths of J&K Tourism

J&K is having better scope in tourism than many states of the country. There are many factors accountable for the huge potential of tourism in the state. Some of them are:

- The state is a well-known destination for its rich cultural heritage, great hospitality and best landscape. Lush green meadows and forests, Mughal gardens, golf course, Dal Lake, Mata Vaishno Devi shrine, Amarnath shrine etc. are some of the famous tourist locations of the state.
- The state is an appropriate destination for different types of tourism which are yet to be exploited like eco-tourism, adventure tourism, medical tourism, polo tourism and leisure tourism.
- Handicrafts of the state like pashmina shawl and paper machie is famous in the whole world.
- Famous Kashmiri food, "wazwan" with its unmatched flavour attracts tourists from every part of the world arriving into the state.
- The local state residents have a lot of experience in tourism related activities.

Tourism and Economy Report of the State

The natural gorgeousness and attractive destinations have made the state a special and privileged spot for tourists across the world. The state is famous for its unique landscape, lakes, gardens, shrines and temples, flora and fauna, forests, high altitude snow laden mountains, glaciers etc. The overall percentage share of tourism industry was 7 percent towards state gross domestic product (SGDP) between 2004-05 and 2012-13. The average number of tourists that arrived in the state was 87,51,669 with average annual growth rate of 11.23 percent.

In terms of share and value, tourism is the chief contributor in overall GSDP and services sector GSDP. As a result, it has been suggested that a better policy needs to be devised at levels whether government or private sector so as to improve the state income (Table 11.1).

Table 11.1: GSDP Contribution of Tourism in Jammu and Kashmir during the Period from 2004-05 to 2012-13

(At constant prices 2004-05) (₹ million)

Year	GSDP	A	I	S	T	Percent share of T in GSDP
2004-05	2730460	610030	770800	1193510	190945	6.99
2005-06	2991990	641060	856080	1324800	205637	7.11
2006-07	3323010	672450	979470	1494900	223651	7.30
2007-08	3709680	706320	1116500	1698610	249482	7.66
2008-09	4231480	742910	1261350	2017440	278736	8.04
2009-10	4838450	815460	1435300	2365770	272839	7.53
2010-11	5697590	938760	1662400	2863970	294836	7.53
2011-12	6597870	1068830	1856860	3426380	293727	7.23
2012-13	7611530	1208000	2017410	4126240	299924	6.95
Average	4636900	822650	1328460	2279070	256642	7.37
Average Annual Growth Rate						
2004-05 to 2012-13	13.88	8.76	13.20	17.40	6.34	-

A = Agriculture; I = Industry; S = Services and T = Tourism

Sources: Centre for Monitoring Indian Economy, New Delhi and Indiastat Database, https:// www. indiastat.com.

In service sectors, the relative share of tourism declined from 15.99 percent in 2004-05 to 7.26 percent in 2012-13 (Table 11.2). However, the sector contributed a major part

(12.50 percent) of service sector GSDP on an average during the period. From agriculture sector, the relative share in overall GSDP declined from 22.34 percent to 15.87 percent during 2004-2013. The share of industry in GSDP reduced from 28.23 percent to 26.5 percent during 2004-2013. Pertinently, the GSDP of the service sector has increased and its relative share in overall GSDP has also increased from 43.71 percent to 54.21 percent during the period. The relative share of tourism increased from 6.99 percent to 8.04 percent during 2008-09, but beyond that there was a decrease in percentage share to 6.95 percent during 2012-13. Therefore, it becomes very essential to take some timely measures for the improvement of state economy and job creation through tourism promotion.

Table 11.2: Relative Shares of Different Sectors in Jammu and Kashmir Economy during 2004-05 to 2012-13

Year	A percent share	I percent share	S percent share	T percent share	Tourism within GSDP Services (percent share)
2004-05	22.34	28.23	43.71	6.99	15.99
2005-06	21.43	28.61	44.28	7.11	15.52
2006-07	20.24	29.48	44.99	7.30	14.96
2007-08	19.04	30.10	45.79	7.66	14.68
2008-09	17.56	29.81	47.68	8.04	13.81
2009-10	16.85	29.66	48.90	7.53	11.53
2010-11	16.48	29.18	50.27	7.53	10.26
2011-12	16.20	28.14	51.93	7.23	8.57
2012-13	15.87	26.50	54.21	6.95	7.26
Average	18.44	28.86	47.97	7.37	12.50

A = Agriculture; I = Industry; S = Services and T = Tourism
Source: Indiastat Database, https://www.indiastat.com.

Between 2004 and 2011, the total number of tourists that arrived in the state were 87,51,669 including both domestic and foreign tourists (Table 11.3). The table shows that arrival of foreign tourists increased from 40,242 in 2004 to 71,593 in 2011 with an average increase of 51,536. The growth rate of foreign tourists arriving during the period was 9.73 percent. On the other side, there was a fluctuating trend in domestic tourist arrival in the state.

Table 11.3: Number of Tourist Arrivals in Jammu and Kashmir during 2004-2011

Year	Foreign tourists	Percent share	Domestic tourists	Percent share	Total tourists
2004	40,242	0.58	68,81,473	99.42	69,21,715
2005	44,345	0.61	72,39,481	99.39	72,83,826
2006	46,087	0.60	76,46,274	99.40	76,92,361
2007	52,754	0.66	79,15,271	99.34	79,68,025
2008	54,697	0.71	76,38,977	99.29	76,93,674
2009	54,475	0.59	92,34,862	99.41	92,89,337
2010	48,099	0.48	99,73,190	99.52	1,00,21,289
2011	71,593	0.54	1,30,71,531	99.46	1,31,43,124
Average	51,537	0.59	8700132	99.41	87,51,669
Average Annual Growth Rates					
2004-12	9.73	--	11.20	--	11.23

Source: Indiastat Database, http://www.indiastat.com.

During the 2004-2011 period, the growth rate of domestic sector was found to be 11.2 percent higher as compared to that of foreigners (9.73 percent) during the period. The above table also shows that the flow of tourists increased from 69,21,715 to 1,31,43,124 between 2004 and 2012 with an annual growth of 11.23 percent. The increase in the flow of tourists is essential to generate economy with a better growth rate. Therefore, it becomes very important for all the stakeholders—both state as well as centre—to share the vision on a single platform with a common goal of tourism growth and development. However, precautionary measures must be taken into consideration for the safety of tourists and the conservation and protection of environment and its resources.

Environmental Impacts

The growth of economy is very important for every nation to explore its resources at the global level. For a country like India, tourism can by no means be underestimated. Tourism helps visitors to get familiar with the customs, culture, tradition, language and style of living of the people. Thus, it helps people from different streams of the society to strengthen their relationship through sharing of culture, tradition, and generosity on a single platform and also makes an easy way to understand international co-operation through business and other commitments. Presently, tourism plays an important role in boosting the economy of India. Therefore, it is very necessary to promote tourism at all levels for the development and prosperity of the nation. In this regard, the Ministry of Tourism at the centre and the Departments of Tourism of the different state governments are in cordial relationship with a view to make all feasible efforts to promote tourism for the sake of a better economy and a prosperous nation.

Tourism has both positive and negative effects. There are a number of positive impacts of tourism which includes growth of economy, jobs, promotion of handicrafts, conservation of heritage places etc. But unfortunately, negative and harmful impacts of tourism also go side by side which deteriorates the nature and the natural resources, threatens the wild life, impacts the habitat and biodiversity, creates pollution etc. Thus, it is very important to maintain the quality of the environment, both natural and man-made for the better tourism and sustained economic development. Tourism and environment have a complex and interdependent relationship with each other. Tourism no doubt plays a key role in the degradation of ecology.

So far as the tourism in Jammu and Kashmir is concerned, it plays a significant role in the growth and development of its economic sector. But along with the positive impacts of tourism in the state, there are a number of negative consequences of tourism as well. These impacts are directly/indirectly linked with the construction of roads, airports, commercial buildings, resorts, shopping malls, hotels, restaurants and golf courses. Unfortunately, the cost of the resulting environmental deterioration due to exploitation of tourism is paid by the local population and most of the time such degradation is observed after some time.

Impact on Water Bodies

Water resources are considered as one of the key attractions for tourism and recreational purposes, but the water bodies are frequently affected by harmful impacts. The deterioration of fresh water resources as a consequence of tourism is very diverse. With the arrival of tourists there is an over exploitation of water resources by hotels etc. which results in shortage and degradation of water supplies along with the generation of waste water, eventually being discharged into the water body. The degree of urban sprawl around the vicinity of Dal Lake influences the water quality because of local population activities and tourist activities in and out of the Dal Lake which ultimately disturbs the aquatic ecosystem through eutrophication and other pollution problems. There is also leakage of fuel and emission of metals, hydrocarbons and other pollutants into the water during boating at Dal Lake. Additionally, there is also heavy siltation and shrinkage of the lake besides degradation of water quality.

It is evident from a number of studies that due to poor management, the urbanization and tourism have adversely affected the quality of water. It has also been observed that there is dumping of municipal and domestic effluents, garbage, excreta and other nutrient rich waste products into Dal Lake. Because of the nutrient enrichment, there is a problem of eutrophication which deteriorates the water quality and degrades the aquatic ecosystem. In the past few decades, industrial waste water and associated heavy metals, agricultural activities, population growth and sewage run-off from urban areas have discharged the nutrients much greater than their natural sources, resulting in an increased growth of blue green algae and weeds due to pollution and eutrophication.

Destruction of Wetlands

Different studies have revealed that wetlands are being exploited illegally by the local population for the construction of houses, roads, hotels, shopping malls and other commercial buildings. Some of the wetlands are forced to induce land use change due to unplanned and irregular urban sprawl.

Impact on Air Quality

The pollution of surrounding atmospheric air is chiefly a result of vehicular traffic, aircrafts and other transportation emissions. The transportation activities, especially in urban centres, are directly interlinked with the number of tourists. The emissions from transport vehicles and energy production and use are the chief factors causing acid rain, global warming and air pollution due to carbon dioxide emissions which ultimately affects air quality and visibility. In comparison to urban areas, the air pollution is less in rural areas due to lesser tourist activities.

Production of Solid Waste

Large quantities of solid waste is being generated in the areas where tourism activities are at large. Tons of waste, garbage, polythene etc. from hotels, restaurants, resorts are being thrown on roads or dumped in water body resulting in sedimentation and unwanted growth of weeds. This problem is more frequently seen in developing countries where waste management technologies and programs are lacking.

Sewage

Sewage is a point source waste which also includes human excreta, generated from houseboats and residential areas, hotels, recreation, tourist spots and other facilities which often lead to sewage pollution. The volume of pollution increases manifold with the increase in tourist arrivals which becomes very difficult to tackle during the peak season of tourism in summers. The sewage pollution threatens the health of flora and fauna and causes severe ill effects on the health of humans and wildlife. It also leads to the growth of algae due to nutrient enrichment which in turn converts fresh water body (oligotrophic) into eutrophic lake.

Threat to Biodiversity and Habitat Loss

The impact of tourism is linked with many activities which include road construction, construction of buildings for commercial purposes, hotels and resorts. Such anthropogenic activities and disproportionate tourism is affecting and threatening the biodiversity and the flora of Kashmir Himalayas. Such biodiversity loss and destruction of habitat along with the destruction of feeding and nesting sites have been reported in many studies due to anthropogenic activities such as construction and development activities for hotels and resorts in Patnitop forests of Jammu and Kashmir.

Besides these negative impacts, there are many more deleterious impacts of tourism in the state of Jammu and Kashmir which include deforestation, soil erosion, vegetation degradation, illegal land occupation, noise pollution, etc. In the past few decades, tourism especially trekking tourism has developed at a rapid rate worldwide in high altitude mountainous regions. In this regard, trekking tourism has been a prime focus for tourists in Ladakh region of the state. Therefore, there is no doubt that mountain tourism is becoming a serious concern for environment especially in developing countries, as confirmed by different studies.

According to recent investigations, it has been found that mountain tourism poses some serious impacts on natural areas, protected areas, and wetlands in developing nations. Trekking, cultural tours, climbing expeditions, river rafting and bird gazing are some typical activities in mountainous regions in developing countries. Such type of tourism leads to physical impacts which include multiple treads, trail widening and incision, soil erosion and compaction and muddiness.

Vegetation trampling and degradation, forest degradation, loss of fragile biodiversity, wildlife disturbance, introduction of exotic species and habitat fragmentation are some biological impacts of trekking tourism. The pollution in surface and sub-surface water caused by dumping of wastes by tourists in the vicinity of camp area leads to serious health problems for the local population. In addition to these negative impacts, trekking activities lead to a number of indirect impacts, such as illegal land occupation, loss of soil, deforestation, off-road driving, vehicular noise pollution, air pollution and other related problems.

Conclusion

Undoubtedly, tourism plays an important role in boosting the economy of J&K state. The tourism has a substantial role in integrating the state with other regions at national and international level. Being an important sector of the J&K economy, tourism contributed around 7 percent of GSDP and 12.50 percent for the services sector both in terms of value and share during the period 2004-05 to 2012-13. Tourism provides new investment opportunities leading to socio-economic development and job opportunities at a large scale besides the overall economic growth of the state. From the other perspective, tourism development is posing a threat to the environment and its resources due to the fragile ecosystem of the state, as well as the lack of adequate basic infrastructure, management policies, and planning tools.

It becomes very difficult to analyze, estimate and assess the impact of tourism as a whole because tourism encompasses a complex network of direct and indirect effects. Development activities related to general infrastructure for tourism include construction of resorts, restaurants, hotels, malls, shops, roads and other commercial units. All these developmental activities are chiefly responsible for the encroachment and degradation of water bodies, agricultural lands, wetlands, forests, and other resources of the state. With the aim for better economic growth and development, there must be judicious use of resources and sustainable development approach of all the stakeholders at all levels viz. regional, national and international.

A framework should be developed in such a way that there should be minimum wastage of resources, minimum pollution of water bodies, less noise and air pollution, minimum waste generation, less impact on biodiversity, forests, soil and other resources. The impacts as a result of tourism growth must be studied, monitored and evaluated in order to support the proposal for better conservation and management of resources, planning policies and regularization of tourist flow. Studies should be taken into consideration at a large scale that would help in addressing the possible impacts and provide a significant contribution to tourism management and planning processes.

Suggestions for Tourism Promotion

From the study, it is revealed that tourism significantly contributes a major part to the state economy, earning valuable foreign exchange and providing job opportunities. However, besides these positive impacts of the tourism industry, there are a number of negative impacts which need to be addressed and resolved. Therefore, the study suggests some positive steps with regard to tourism development and protection of the environment in J&K state.

1. Maximum support of the government at both the State and the Central level for better economic growth and development.
2. A well documented tourism policy that provides equal opportunities to all stake holders (local population, NGOs and the private sector) related to tourism industry.
3. Proper planning and related measures with respect to the number of tourists coming to the state according to the carrying capacity.
4. Infrastructure development with regard to tourism is lacking. Therefore, development of general infrastructure should be done for tourism related activities in order to handle the tourist flow with care and hospitality. Keeping in mind the protection of environment, infrastructure should not further deteriorate the natural resources, biodiversity, forests, soil, water bodies etc.
5. Proper planning and policies should be made so that there is minimum degradation of the environment. Degraded

water bodies, forest regions, infrastructure and other landscape must be restored in order to increase the quality of the environment.

Thus, in order to avoid the negative impacts of tourism, there is a need for proper planning and management and plans and policies for all the stake holders for better economic growth and a sustainable environment.

References

Ahmad, W.M. (2016), "Study on Dal Lake of Kashmir with Special Reference to the Different Pollutants and Their Control Measures".

Andereck, K.L. (1993), "Impacts of Tourism on Natural Resources", *Parks and Recreation (Arlington)*, 28(6), pp. 26-86.

Beeton, S. (2006), "Community Development through Tourism", Landlinks Press.

Buckley, R.C., Pickering, C.M. and Warnken, J. (2000), "Environmental Management for Alpine Tourism and Resorts in Australia", *Tourism and Development in Mountain Regions*, pp. 27-45.

Buntaine, M.T., Mullen, R.B. and Lassoie, J.P. (2007), "Human Use and Conservation Planning in Alpine Areas of North-western Yunnan, China", *Environment, Development and Sustainability*, 9(3), pp. 305-324.

Chatterjea, K. (2007), "Assessment and Demarcation of Trail Degradation in a Nature Reserve, Using GIS: Case of Bukit Timah Nature Reserve", *Land Degradation and Development*, 18(5), pp. 500-518.

Dar, G.H., and Naqshi, A.R. (2002), "Plant Resources of Kashmir: Diversity, Utilization and Conservation", Valley Book House, Srinagar, Kashmir, pp. 109-122.

Dokulil, M.T. (2014), "Environmental Impacts of Tourism on Lakes", in 'Eutrophication: Causes, Consequences and Control', Springer, Netherlands, pp. 81-88.

Fazal, S. and Amin, A. (2011), "Impact of Urban Land Transformation on Water Bodies in Srinagar City, India", *Journal of Environmental Protection*, 2(2), pp. 142-153.

Gadoo, M. (2011), "Role of Tourism in the Economic Development of Jammu and Kashmir: A Case Study of Tourism Department",

M. Phil. Dissertation, University of Kashmir.

Gonsalves, D.V. and D'Souza, J. (1999), "Impact of Tourism Industry on Ground Water in Calangute, Goa", *Ecology Environment and Conservation*, 5, pp. 19-24.

Holden, A. (2009), "An Introduction to Tourism-Environment Relationships", *Ecotourism and Environmental Sustainability Principles and Practice*, pp. 583-592.

Hutchinson, G.E. (1973), "Marginalia: Eutrophication: The Scientific Background of a Contemporary Practical Problem", *American Scientist*, 61(3), pp. 269-279.

Kanth, T.A. and Yousuf Bhat, M. (1997), "Environmental Impact Assessment of Tourism: A Case Study of Dal Lake Kashmir", *Transactions of the Institute of Indian Geographers*, 19(2), pp. 63-74.

Kim, K. (2002), "The Effects of Tourism upon Quality of Life of Residents in the Community", doctoral dissertation.

Koussouris, T. and Diapoulis, A. (1989), "Mikri Prespa Lake: Ecological Changes from Natural and Anthropogenic Causes", *Toxicological and Environmental Chemistry*, 20(1), pp. 49-52.

Lankford, S.V. and Howard, D.R. (1994), "Developing a Tourism Impact Attitude Scale", *Annals of Tourism Research*, 21, pp. 121-139.

Leung, Y.F. and Marion, J.L. (2000), "Recreation Impacts and Management in Wilderness: A State of Knowledge Review", Wilderness Science in a Time of Change Conference, pp. 23-48.

Luo, G., Bu, F., Xu, X., Cao, J. and Shu, W. (2011), "Seasonal Variations of Dissolved Inorganic Nutrients Transported to the Linjiang Bay of the Three Gorges Reservoir, China", *Environmental Monitoring and Assessment*, 173(1), pp. 55-64.

Malik, Ab. R., Bhat, A.H. and Bhat, F.A. (2013), "Impact of Tourism on Environmental Conditions of Jammu and Kashmir", *International Journal of Advanced Research in Economics and Commerce,* 1(1), pp. 1-9.

Marion, J. L. and Leung, Y.F. (2001), "Trail Resource Impacts and an Examination of Alternative Assessment Techniques", *Journal of Park and Recreation Administration*, 19(3), pp. 17-37.

Mir, H.A. (2014), "Impact of Tourism Industry on Economic Development of Jammu and Kashmir", *International Journal of*

Scientific and Engineering Research, 5(6), pp. 592-598.

Monz, C. (2000), "Recreation Resource Assessment and Monitoring Techniques for Mountain Regions", *Tourism and Development in Mountain Regions*, pp. 255-274.

Moss, L.A. and Godde, P.M. (2000), "Strategy for Future Mountain Tourism", *Tourism and Development in Mountain Regions*, pp. 323-338.

Pandotra, A. and Sahi, D.N. (2013), "Species Composition and Status of Avifauna of Patnitop: A Sub-temperate Forest Habitat of Jammu (J&K)", *Journal of Biosphere*, 2(1), pp. 59-61.

Price, M.F. (1992), "Patterns of the Development of Tourism in Mountain Environments", *Geo Journal*, 27(1), pp. 87-96.

Rabbany, M.G., Afrin, S., Rahman, A., Islam, F. and Hoque, F. (2013), "Environmental Effects of Tourism", *American Journal of Environment, Energy and Power Research*, 1(7), pp. 117-130.

Rashid, H. and Naseem, G. (2007), "Quantification of Loss in Spatial Extent of Lakes and Wetlands in the Suburbs of Srinagar City during the Last Century Using Geospatial Approach", The 12th World Lake Conference, pp. 653-658.

Saffery, A. (2000), "Mongolia's Tourism Development Race: Case Study from the Gobi Gurvansaikhan National Park", *Tourism and Development in Mountain Regions*, pp. 255-274.

Shah, J.J., Nagpal, T. and Brandon, C. (eds.) (1997), "Urban Air Quality Management Strategy in Asia: Guidebook", World Bank Publications.

Sharma, A. and Raina, A.K. (2014), "Environmental Impacts of Tourism in Katra Town (J&K)", *International Journal of Innovative Research in Science, Engineering and Technology*, 3(6).

Sheldon, P.J. and Var, T. (1984), "Resident Attitudes to Tourism in North Wales", *Tourism Management,* 5(1), pp. 40-47.

Singh, K. and Unjum, I. (2016), "Tourism in Jammu and Kashmir Economy: Role and Performance", *Journal of Economic and Social Development*, 12(2), pp. 112-123.

Stevens, S. (2003), "Tourism and Deforestation in the Mt. Everest Region of Nepal", *The Geographical Journal*, 169(3), pp. 255-277.

Sunlu, U. (2003), "Environmental Impacts of Tourism", Conference on the Relationships between Global Trades and Local Resources in the Mediterranean Region.

Tali, B.A., Ganie, A.H., Nawchoo, I.A., Wani, A.A. and Reshi, Z.A. (2015), "Assessment of Threat Status of Selected Endemic Medicinal Plants Using IUCN Regional Guidelines: A Case Study from Kashmir Himalaya", *Journal for Nature Conservation*, 23, pp. 80-89.

Tonderayi, D. (2000), "Amenity Migration and Tourism in the Eastern Highland Bioregion of Zimbabwe: Policy Planning and Management Considerations", Tourism and Development in Mountain Regions. Wallingford: CABI Publishing, pp. 297-322.

Vaugeois, N. (2000), "Tourism in Developing Countries: Refining a Useful Tool for Economic Development", Proceedings of 6th World Leisure Congress, Bilbao, Spain.

Zan, F., Huo, S., Xi, B., Su, J., Li, X., Zhang, J. and Yeager, K.M. (2011), "A 100 Year Sedimentary Record of Heavy Metal Pollution in a Shallow Eutrophic Lake, Lake Chaohu, China", *Journal of Environmental Monitoring*, 13(10), pp. 2788-2797.

12

Promotion of Tourism in Punjab: Problems and Prospects

Harpreet Kaur

Why is Tourism Important?

Tourism sector has a major role to play to promote faster, sustainable and more inclusive economic growth. It has better prospects for promoting pro-poor growth than many other sectors. This is because tourism involves a collection of activities, services and industries comprising transportation, accommodation, eating and drinking establishments, retail shops, entertainment businesses and other hospitality services provided to individuals or groups travelling away from home for leisure, business or other purposes. The broad scope of economic activities involved enables wider participation in its growth, including participation by the informal sector. Tourism is also highly dependent upon natural capital (mountains, forests, rivers, lakes, wildlife) and culture and these are the assets that some of the poor have, even if they have no financial resources. For all these reasons, across the world, the tourism industry is one of the largest generators of employment.

In India, tourism sector is based on exploiting its unique endowments of biodiversity, forests, rivers, and its rich culture and heritage. The challenges in this sector lie in successfully preserving these in their original form, and making them accessible to domestic and international travellers. Tourism in India has the potential to create economic interest of local communities in the protection of its natural and cultural endowments leading to a more *sustainable growth.*

Sustainable Tourism

While tourism is important for both growth and employment generation, it must also be sustainable. The World Tourism Organization (WTO) has defined sustainable tourism as 'leading to management of all resources in such a way that economic, social and aesthetic needs can be fulfilled while maintaining cultural integrity, essential ecological processes, biological diversity and life support systems'. In 1992, the Earth Summit in Rio established the triple principles of environmental, economic and social sustainability. Since then, the principles of sustainable tourism have been adopted by the tourism industry worldwide.

The traditional approach to tourism development is a direct result of an extremely open and deregulated world economic environment. This approach is characterised by inequity in redistribution of economic benefits. Over the years, new non-traditional approaches (like eco-tourism) which are concerned more with ecological and cultural conservation than poverty reduction have become popular. The aim is more on minimizing the costs on people's lives rather than bringing benefits to them.

Pro-poor Tourism

Any strategy to promote tourism should emphasise the need to adopt a *pro-poor tourism* approach aimed at increasing the net benefits to the poor from tourism and ensure that tourism growth contributes to poverty reduction. The benefits may be economic, social, environmental or cultural. For this purpose, there is a need for developing a comprehensive set of strategies for a diversity of actions, from micro to macro level, including product and infrastructure development, marketing, branding and promotion, planning, policy and investment and increasing the spread of benefits to the weaker sections. To realize the tourism potential of India's enormous assets—namely historical sites, places of religious significance, and its vast range of national attractions—the focus must be on developing clusters or circuits around such assets. The development of these clusters/circuits requires collaboration between many agencies at the local level to create an attractive and safe transit experience. Therefore, development of tourism requires States take a leading role in developing their own tourism potential to achieve growth in employment and income.

Tourism in Punjab

Punjab state of India has very attractive religious places and heritage sites, which attract international, national and domestic tourists and has major potential to become a global tourist destination. There are three principal Takhts of Sikhs in Punjab. Moreover, there are many important Hindu temples, which have a history behind them, such as the Ram Tirath and Durgiana Mandir at Amritsar and Kali Devi Mandir at Patiala. Two major tourism destinations of Punjab are Amritsar and Anandpur Sahib. During 2009, the State ranked at 28th (in terms of arrival of domestic tourists) by the Ministry of Tourism, Government of India. It was ranked 14th amongst the States in 2010 and 12th in 2011. The number of domestic tourist visits increased from 1,05,83,509 in 2010 to 1,64,16,638 in 2011.

In the year 2008, UNWTO had formulated a tourism development master plan for the period encompassing 2008-2023. The Master Plan recognised the potential of Punjab to become a competitive tourism destination based on its rich cultural, religious and natural heritage. However, the State government has not executed any concerted effort to develop tourism in a planned manner in Punjab (Chadha and Choudhary, 2016).

The first state tourism policy was formulated in the year 1999 and tourism was given the status of an industry in the Ninth Five Year Plan (1997-2002). Tourism policy incorporates features like socio-economic benefits, employment generation, eco-friendliness and simultaneously aims at fulfilling the growing demand for tourism products in the state brought due to rapid industrial development. Punjab government prepared a plan to attract tourists to the state with the help of UNWTO, which is known for its craftsmanship, folk dances, cuisine and the holy shrines. Punjab government has identified tourism as the third most important sector after agriculture and manufacturing (Chadha and Choudhary, 2016).

It has made huge investments in developing infrastructure, marketing and publicity of tourist sites, monuments, developing tourism products, historical and religious buildings and the hotel sector.

Literature Review

Due to the prospective economic benefits of tourism like enhanced incomes, employment, foreign exchange earnings, taxes etc., many governments have engaged in tourism development for the purpose of promoting economic growth. The relationship between tourism and economic development has been an admired topic in recent tourism literature. However, researchers have reached sometimes conflicting and mixed results despite the common choice of time series techniques as a research methodology. It has long been recognized that tourism does have a positive impact on the economic activity. Tourism is known to have important and beneficial impacts on economic situation. A fast-paced development of the tourism sector results in an increase in household income as well as government revenues through multiplier effects. Progress in the balance of payments and growth in the number of tourism-related government policies works on relationship between tourism and economic growth in a cross-country setting. Empirical results include reverse causality, non-linearity and interactive effects.

Objectives and Methodology

The consent is that tourism has been pivotal in social progress as well as has been an important vehicle of widening socio-economic and cultural contacts throughout human history. Over the past years, many developing and developed countries have considered tourism as an option for sustainable development of their nations. The importance of tourism as a contributor to economic growth is so widely accepted that year after year throughout the world, massive investments continue to pour in its development. In this context, the objective of present study is to evaluate the existing situation of the growth of Punjab's tourism as an introduction to its supplementary promotional programmes.

Also, the study assesses the regional policies suggesting actions for promotion of healthy and area- friendly tourism in Punjab. The present study is based on the secondary data provided by various agencies and organizations, analysis of such appropriate reports of Tourism Development Corporation, newspapers, previous studies, plans and other documentation, together with discussions made within the tourism authorities.

Current Status of Tourism in Punjab

Availability of accommodation facilities for tourists is not satisfactory in Punjab. Punjab is full of roadside *dhabas*, which provide authentic Punjabi cuisine at very cheap prices and at the same time, a number of small hotels and guesthouses are also scattered all over the state. As per Ministry of Tourism data, as on October 31, 2010, there were a total of 112 approved category hotels having 3,235 rooms in different categories in Punjab state (Table 12.1).

Assessment after the 2008 policy suggests that the number of recognized inbound tour operators, travel agencies, tourist transport operators, and adventure tour operators were very less and even nil in two categories. Table 12.2 shows that no skilled guides were available which surely is a hindrance for the foreign tourists. However a large number of non-registered tour operators, travel agents and tourist transport operators can be seen in many parts of Punjab. This basically suggests that the data available may not be authentic enough.

Table 12.1 Category-wise Number of Approved Hotels and Rooms in Punjab

Star Category	No. of Hotels	No. of Rooms
5 Star Deluxe	2	365
5-Star	2	178
4-Star	7	358
3-Star	55	1588
2-Star	44	717
1-Star	2	29
Total	112	3235

Source: Ministry of Tourism, Government of India.

Table 12.2: Tourist Guides Availability

State	Inbound tour operators	Travel agencies	Tourist transport operators	Adventure tour operators	Domestic tour operators
Punjab	01	14	3	Nil	Nil

Source: India Tourism Statistics, 2010.

Tourist Arrivals

Tables 12.3 and 12.4 portray the data depicting the number of tourist arrivals. Most of the tourists visited Amritsar. Number of domestic visitors was more than the foreign ones.

Current Challenges of Tourism Promotion in Punjab

- **Inadequate Infrastructure**: Bottlenecks in infrastructure, less options of tourist guest houses and hotels, less affordable and reliable communication network, conditions of roads, marketing strategies and most importantly lack of proper policy on tourism development due to least interest by the state governments are all hindering the expected development and promotion of tourism in the state.

Table 12.3: Tourist Arrivals in the State and in Amritsar

Year	Punjab	Amritsar
2009	54,80,399	22,58,402
2010	1,07,20,631	48,85,865
2011	1,65,67,596	1,10,96,952
2012	1,91,19,943	1,00,72,719
2013	2,15,44,962	1,20,58,034
2014	2,45,26,751	1,53,68,340
2015	2,60,38,728	1,69,24,412
2016	3,93,63,061	2,54,62,627

Source: punjabtourism.gov.in (2017)

Table 12.4: Domestic and Foreign Tourist Arrivals in Punjab

Year	Domestic	Foreign	Total
2009	53,69,995	1,10,404	54,80,399
2010	1,05,83,509	1,37,122	1,07,20,631
2011	1,64,16,638	1,50,958	1,65,67,596
2012	1,90,56,143	1,43,805	1,91,19,943
2013	2,13,40,888	2,04,074	2,15,44,962
2014	2,42,71,302	2,55,449	2,45,26,751
2015	2,57,96,361	2,42,367	2,60,38,728
2016	3,87,03,325	6,59,736	3,93,63,061

Source: punjabtourism.gov.in (2017).

- **Lack of Coordinated Efforts:** There is a lack of coordination among several departments like Department of Tourism and Department of Archaeology in managing the demands of the tourists in places of both religious and historic importance. There is virtually no coordination between various public industries and private sector like Punjab Tourism Development Corporation as well Haryana Tourism Development Corporation. This is definitely a major hurdle in the way of development of tourism industry.
- **Absence of Tourist Guides:** Punjab does not have any trained guides placed at important places of tourist

attraction. Consequently, when the tourists arrive at such a place there is hardly anyone to satisfy the curiosity of the tourists. The Department of Tourism started a program to train tourist guides. But these efforts did not yield good results as most of the trainees left the job. Some of them found other means of livelihood while others found it to be less paying because of the poor inflow of tourists in the state.

- **Perception about Law and Order:** The media often tends to focus on the ethnic conflicts and under development of the State neglecting the pioneering development efforts made in the region. It has been engraved in the minds of the public by the media that there is a law and order problem and unsafe environment for tourists, especially foreign tourists and women in the state. The foreign as well as domestic tourists think it is risky to visit the state, in view of the prevailing law and order situation. The most effective way of removing this negative intuition is by assuring full safety and cooperation by the local administration.
- **Under-developed Human Resources:** As discussed in previous paragraphs, tour operators, hoteliers, transporters, tourist guides etc. are not trained enough to provide detailed information to the tourists regarding the region which obviously is a barrier in the path of development of tourism industry in the state.

Thus, despite abundance of religious places, cultural and historical places, the flow of incoming tourists has been marginal for the reasons cited above.

Policy Implications

The Government of Punjab can organize youth and cultural exchange programs for the domestic tourists from neighbouring States. One may also suggest a 'joint regional advertisement and publicity' with a view to promote travel to the region.

Physical infrastructure and other infrastructural services,

including multi-level car parking, traffic management, state of the banking facilities, mobile dispensaries, general cleanliness of the places of stay and food and catering services need to be upgraded.

Government expenditure on tourism promotion should be increased, as it was very less in the annual plans of the Punjab government.

For tapping the optimal tourism potential, particularly of domestic tourists, a proper record of the vacation schedule of administrative and educational institutions in different regions of the country should be maintained.

Tourism promotion and publicity should be stepped up during the vacation time by offering special holiday packages for the potential tourists.

Conclusion

A lot of things are being said and promised in context of tourism development in the state. However, while actually visiting these places, not much is evident from the prevailing conditions. Tourism in present day does not confine itself to hotels, restaurants and sea beaches. Its broad arena touches upon rural areas, health sector and the environment. The new approach is to position tourism as a major engine of growth for employment generation and economic development. There is thus an urgent need to position Punjab as an international brand like Kerala i.e. 'Gods own country' and include the State into the highly successful "Incredible India" campaign. If tourism is developed through careful planning, it is sure to bring revolutionary transformation in the state economy. Initiatives and incentives by the government will add advantage in promoting tourism in the state which not only will help in economic development but also in the promotion of socio-cultural character of the state.

References

Arslanturk, Y., Balcilar, M., Ozdemir, Z.A. (2011), "Time-varying Linkages between Tourism Receipts and Economic Growth in a Small Open Economy", *Economic Modelling*, 28, pp. 664-671.

Balaguer, J. and Cantavella, M. (2002), "Tourism as a Long-run Economic Growth Factor: The Spanish Case", *Applied Economics*, 34, pp. 877-884.

Brohman, J. (1996), "New Directions in Tourism for Third World Development", *Annals of Tourism Research*, 23, pp. 48-70.

Chadha, N. and Choudhary, P. (2016), Nature, Problems and Prospects of Rural Tourism in Punjab: An Analysis" *Pacific Business Review International,* 1.

Donald, M.M. (2007), "Evaluation Study of Rural Tourism Scheme", submitted to the M.R. division, Ministry of Tourism, Government of India.

Dwyer, L., Forsyth, P. and Spurr, R. (2004), "Evaluating Tourism's Economic Effects: New and Old Approaches", *Tourism Management,* 25, pp. 307-317.

Gantzer, H. and Gantzer, C. (1983), "Managing Tourists and Politicians in India", *Tourism Management,* pp. 118- 125.

Lim, C. (1987), "Review of International Tourism Demand Models", *Annals of Tourism Research*, 2 (4), pp. 835-849.

Malik, M.M. and Nusrath, A. (2014), "A Review of Tourism Development in India", *Golden Research Thoughts,* 3, p. 11.

Patel, R. (2012), "India's Tourism Industry: Progress and Emerging Issues", *Arth Prabhand: A Journal of Economics and Management*.

13

Social Responsibility, Tourism and Sustainable Development

Amandeep Kaur and Jubilee Padmanabhan

Introduction

India is a great country from the perspectives of prosperity of different historical, religious and cultural places in various regions. Due to this, tourism in India is mounting day by day and becoming the means of national benefits. Hence, the government is more attentively taking a part in the maintenance and development of tourism. It is very difficult to manage such things and there are lots of challenges and barriers that are essential to overcome. The problems such as poor transportation facilities; lacuna of sanitized services at the different places of tourist interest; non-standardization or unfairness of charges and fares; lack of maintenance of cultural and heritage goods and places; problems related to security and harassment; lack of promotion about different tourist places; scarcity of trained employees; administrative and management skills, untrained guides; excessive formalities for taking permission to visit the restricted areas; lack of concerns about the growth of village tourism; scarcity of supportive infrastructure such as roads, drinking water facilities, health and environmental sanitation etc. create frequent hurdles in the ways of Indian tourism (Patel, 2012).

In addition to these, the most crucial points to be discussed in this context are the development of concerns of social responsibility and the expansion of sustainable development among every individual. It is very common that the people, who organize, maintain and run tourism, often breach social norms and ethics. Due to this, the local people and foreigners face a lot of problems and social responsibility of such tourism agencies becomes questionable.

Social Responsibility and its Relation to Tourism

Social responsibility in tourism is considered as taking responsibility for all the activities and following the principles that can be modified and applied despite the benefits of the business. It is mostly emphasizing on maximizing the positive effects and minimizing the negative effects on society (customers, owners, employees, community, suppliers, government). Since, tourism is considered as a business, the term corporate social responsibility (CSR) is used in this stream which was coined by H. Bowen in 1953.

Corporate social responsibility (CSR) refers to the integration and consideration of social and environmental issues with the decisions, goals and operations of business. Other terms such as corporate responsibility, sustainability, corporate citizenship and ethical business practices are used for corporate social responsibility interchangeably. In India, it was introduced under the Companies Act, 2013.

There are many different factors that enhance the interest of tourism organizing agencies towards corporate social responsibility such as, globalization, customers' demands of good products and services, influence of international organizations such as United Nations (UN), Organization for Economic Co-operation and Development (OECD), International Labour Organization (ILO) and the need for sustainable development.

There are three types of social responsibilities viz. legal, ethical and economic. The *legal* dimension of corporate social responsibility (CSR) deals with the compliance of laws and regulations which are established by the authorities and set standards of responsible behaviour according to the requirements and expectations of the society. Consumer protection laws, environmental laws and laws that promote safety and fairness come under legal corporate social responsibility. The second type of social responsibility is *ethical* CRS, which is related to such behaviours and activities that are permitted or prohibited by organization members and society. It is not essential that these activities should be codified by law. These do's and don'ts are more related to the honesty and truthfulness of the person rather than the compliance of any law or rules and regulations. To enhance ethical consideration in tourism, it is mandatory that organizations and companies should address ethical issues from its very foundation and include them in their business strategy.

The ethical issues include activities such as, environmental and cultural protection, maintaining social equality, and genuineness and truthfulness while explaining historical places and fares to foreign tourists.

Economic dimension of CSR is related to the ways in which resources are circulated within the social system for the production and construction of goods and services. Economy is also dependent upon the relationships between environment and corporations. In tourism, the major environmental concerns are water, soil and air pollution. Controlling and minimizing pollution consumes a lot of economic and labour efforts. So, there is a need to encourage and establish mechanisms in these organizations that focus on control of pollution and other environment friendly policies. In addition to this, equal employment opportunities, health and safety at work, job diversity, and employees' privacy are some major concerns in economic social responsibility.

The consideration of corporate social responsibility (CSR) by the organizing agencies and companies benefits the clients, society and the organizers themselves. Due to social responsibility, the reputation, competitiveness, productivity and employer's motivation have increased to greater extent. On the other hand, corporate social responsibility (CSR) also helps in providing better and expected conditions for the target groups, identification of new problematic or challenging areas and development of new approaches to solve these problems.

Principles of Social Responsibility in Tourism

To maintain social responsibility in tourism, it is essential to follow three main principles, i.e. sustainability, accountability and transparency.

The principle of *sustainability* refers to fulfilling and continuing such activities that have a positive effect on the future. According to this principle, the services that the tourism organizing agencies are providing today should be present after at least five years with same quality and quantity. However, it is not possible to every context because, the natural resources are decreasing day by day and we should look for alternative ways to tackle this problem.

There should be emphasis on waste reduction, reuse and recycling of such resources. The members of tourism organizing agencies should cooperate and be in touch with the local recycling coordinators, state and federal regulators, environmental educators, consumers and waste management professionals.

The second principle of social responsibility is *accountability* which is related to the responsibility of the employees of these agencies for providing trustable services and good practices. The accountability motivates and enhances the sense of social responsibility among employees.

The third principle of *transparency* deals with clarity and publicly displaying the list of roles, responsibilities, ethical issues to be concerned, rules and regulations of the organization and its boards and management committee. Transparency should be a part of every agency as it facilitates the social responsibility and accountability too. A certain amount of transparency helps to cultivate good practices among the educated, active and loyal public. It also leads to more efficient quality of management and consumers receive better products and services according to their needs and expectations.

Tourism and Sustainable Development

Another burning issue of tourism is the sustainable development which is extremely important to be considered.

Sustainable development recognizes that, progress of society must be both inclusive and environment friendly which fulfils the requirements and brings prosperity for present generation without compromising on the needs of the future generation. Sustainable development has a three-dimensional approach that focus on the preservation of economic, environmental and cultural (social) resources not for a short-term but for the long-term needs which should followed by every country.

Likewise, sustainable development in tourism means taking into consideration the current and future economic, social and environmental effects of tourism, addressing the needs of tourists, industry, environment and communities of the host country. The main focus of sustainable development in tourism is on using the available social, economic and environmental resources in ways that will have minimum negative effect on the present and future generations.

As tourism industry in India is swiftly developing day by day, the amount of consumption of economic and environmental resources is also increasing rapidly. About 88.90 lakh foreign tourists arrived in India in 2016 registering a 10.7 percent growth from the previous year. Therefore, it is obvious that, this large quantum has influence on the social, economic and environmental aspects of the country. Its larger effects can be seen on the social aspect of every country. Violation of human rights, criminality, prostitution, alcohol, drug abuse and child labour has increased in many countries due to tourism. International Labour Organization (ILO) estimates that 3 million and 19 million children and teenagers work in the tourism sector respectively.

Besides these, cultural diversity is another problematic area. Tourism provides a channel from traditional lifestyle to modern or Western way of living. Accordingly, it has also influenced the behavioural trends and norms of countries, due to which cultural conflicts arise and harm the traditional value system of the host community.

All these social issues should be considered seriously and

appropriate steps should be taken to resolve the same. For this, it is very necessary that investors and tourists do not engage or promote child labour, prostitution or any other kind of exploitation. Moreover, it is more appropriate that the tourism organizing companies participate in global campaign against such violation of human rights. There should be some projects or tourist training programs for the tourists that help in educating them about the cultural heritage, ways of living, history and code of conduct of a specific region or country before and after their arrival at that place.

Sustainable Practices in Promoting Tourism

The environmental problems that are sprouting from tourism are also multifarious. The organizers and tourists have lacuna of knowledge and awareness of how to use natural resources sustainably. Consequently, this often leads to over consumption and degradation of resources. The major environmental harm and wastage of resources that tourism generates is wastage of water, energy and food; solid waste; air and soil pollution; sewage problems and climate change. It is estimated that 72 percent CO_2 emissions come from transportation, 24 percent from accommodation, and 4 percent from local activities. Aviation industry alone stands to contribute 55 percent of these transportation CO_2 emissions out of which 40 percent is related to tourism activities.

To reduce these environmental hazards in present and future, the awareness and sensitivity of tourists and organizers towards sustainable development is indispensable. The organizers or investors should stress upon the use of environmentally sound technologies or alternative ways to minimize the consumption of resources. The water can be saved by using water saving equipments and by collecting and using rain water. Proper sewage system should also be maintained by the organizers. Along with this, organic and non-organic garbage must be treated separately by using appropriate waste disposal systems. It is also important to use ecological materials and installation of renewable sources of energy systems such as solar energy, wind power in the residential areas of tourists. The preservation and appropriate use of such natural resources also fulfil the economic aims of sustainable development of tourism in India.

Human Resources Development for Tourism

As in some other service sectors, there is a large skill deficit in the tourism sector, which is impeding its development and impinging on its competitiveness.

The Indian Institute of Travel and Tourism Management (IITTM) is an institute affiliated to the All India Council for Technical Education, running courses for tour operators and holding examinations and granting diploma. The IITTM also conducts short-term courses for tour guides, holds examinations and grants diplomas for the profession.

Tourism is a labour-intensive industry and a major source of employment. Therefore, issues of human resources development and capacity building are extremely important. The problem of human resources is identified as shortage of trained labour, lack of trainers, inadequate training materials and lack of tourism education strategies as part of national tourism planning. Other issues concerning human resources development in the tourism industry include working conditions, availability of education and training policy issues, information technology and cultural issues.

Developing human resources in the tourism sector faces unique challenges because customer preferences, travel patterns, information technology and conditions at destinations are changing rapidly. As a result, strong and flexible human resource development strategies are needed. The strategy should mirror human resource needs and the corresponding recruitment, employment and training requirements.

Training programmes need to articulate well with employment creation for maximum synergy. Training should be strictly need-based. Thus, it is necessary to establish linkages with various labour market institutions and processes viz. labour market information, employment services, public works, credit and other support to small enterprises, unemployment and social support services and so on. Training services for existing enterprises to upgrade and re-orient technical skills or develop management capacity can help stimulate their labour absorption, avoid retrenchments and facilitate redeployment of retrenched workers. Therefore, the tourism training strategy should focus on employability, sustainability and promotion of decent work culture especially to safeguard foreign tourists.

Tourist Clusters

In affluent countries there is a flow of tourists out of the cities not only during holidays but almost every weekend. The weekend tourists, particularly those with children, normally go out short distances to resorts and tourist destinations, such as mountains, lakes and beaches. Additionally, they also go to man made attractions and clusters of other attractions.

The rapid increase in disposable income in the upper middle class in India presents a big opportunity for the development of tourism in the country.

Efforts should be made for the creation of tourism clusters of areas between 100 and 500 acres within a distance of 150 kilometres from the cities for the setting up of a cluster of facilities and attractions for tourism. They may have hotels, restaurants, spas, theme parks like Appu Ghar in Delhi and Essel World in Mumbai, and attractions such as skating rings, lakes with boating and sailing facilities, golf courses, tennis courts, and indoor games. Although the clientele of tourist clusters will primarily be domestic, they will also serve to increase the attractiveness of traditional tourist destinations for international tourists.

Centre-State Co-ordination

In terms of the federal framework of the Constitution, the

responsibilities of the Union Government and the State Governments are elaborated in separate schedules to the Constitution.

The Central Government is responsible for matters such as external affairs, visa regulations, foreign exchange regulations and import/export procedures, while the State Governments are responsible, *inter alia*, for law and order, land use, civic amenities, shops and establishments. These governments have separate agencies for dealing with specific subjects and regulations. For example, the Ministry of Tourism in the Union Government is concerned with the overall coordination and planning of tourism development in the country and for undertaking tourism promotion and publicity in the international market. However, the State governments control all factors of production including land in their territories. Further, there is empirical evidence to suggest that a significant proportion of their tax revenues are attributable to consumption by tourists.

Therefore, the State Governments have the responsibility and the incentive for facilitating the creation of infrastructure for tourism. The role of the Union Government is restricted to establishing a policy and regulatory framework, creating the appropriate incentive structure and synergising the activities of different infrastructure sectors across levels of government and supplementing these efforts by financial assistance.

Conclusion

Nowadays, tourism industry is expanding rapidly and becoming a strong means of national economy. Due to lack of awareness and sensitivity of tourists and investors about the environmental, social and economic influence of tourism, the perspectives of social responsibility and sustainable development are crucial to be considered. There is a need for accountability and transparency in the services provided by the industry in regard to implementing and following ethics, code of conduct and social responsibility in total. Moreover, tourists should be responsible for maintaining and respecting the cultural and social heritage of the host country. Along with this, State and Central governments should have check on the services of such industries. In a nutshell, it can be said that if tourism organizers understand and believe in the statement that 'leading a business is more than just making a profit' then the issues related to social responsibility and sustainable development can be solved to a greater extent.

References

Arnaudova, K. and Koseska, E. (2012), "Business Ethics and Social Responsibility in Tourist Organizations in Terms of Changing Environment", *Procedia Social and Behavioral Sciences*, 44, pp. 387-397.

Hiralal, M. (2015), "India's Corporate Social Responsibility", Indian Companies Act, 2013.

Jucan, C.N. and Jucan, M.S. (2010), "Social Responsibility in Tourism and Sustainable Development", *WSEAS Transactions on Environment and Development*, 10(6).

Khan, S. (2015), "Ethics in Tourism", available at: https://www.slideshare.net/shahrukhkh/ethics-in-tourism.

Lyon, T.P. and Maxwell, J.W. (2008), "Corporate Social Responsibility and the Environment: A Theoretical Perspective", *Review of Environmental Economics and Policy Advance Access*, 1, pp. 1-22.

Patel, R. (2012), "India's Tourism Industry: Progress and Emerging Issues", *Journal of Economics and Management*, 1(5).

Peeters, P. and Dubois, G. (2010), "Tourism Travel under Climate Change Mitigation Constraints", *Journal of Transport Geography*, 18 (3), pp. 447-457.

"Performance of Tourism Sector during March 2016", (2016), Ministry of Tourism, Government of India.

Sharma, S., Sharma, J. and Devi, A. (2009), "Corporate Social Responsibility: The Key Role of Human Resources", *Management Business Intelligence Journal*, 2(1), pp. 205-213.

14

Social Value Creation through Development of Tourism

Sandeep and Shamshir Singh Dhillon

Introduction

The term *value* is tremendously elusive and complex. Michael Haralambos says "A value is a belief that something is good and worthwhile. It defines what is worth having and worth striving". G.R. Leslie, R.F. Larson, H.L. Gorman opine, "values are group conceptions of the relative desirability of things". The word value is generally taken in economic sense that means the price of a thing.

However, there is value in the moral, political, and/or cultural sense, which is of course somewhat different from the monetary-based understanding of value that might spring to mind when one hears the word 'value'. Values are the criteria people use in assessing their daily lives; arrange their priorities and choosing between alternative courses of action. In late 1920s, values were defined as basic interests or motives in the personality of an individual. Spranger in his book "Type of Man" classified values among six categories: The Theoretical: whose dominant interest is the discovery of truth; The Economic: who is interested in what is useful particularly related with the money; The Aesthetic: whose highest value is form and harmony; The Social: whose highest value is love of people; The Political: whose interest is primarily in power; and The Religious: whose highest value is unity. Ultimately, value refers to the ways in which one chooses to represent the importance of a particular idea, object, action, or place.

Social Values

Social value is different from the meaning of value in economics. Social values are the values that are of common interest for the development of society. These are the values that are being held by the people of that society. These are deep rooted in their mind due to the long practices of them and ethical importance attached to them that they have been witnessing for ages. These social values account for the stability of social order. These provide the general guidelines for social conduct. "Social values are moral beliefs and principles that are accepted by the majority so as to ensure the continuity of a society". The origin of these beliefs and principles is found in the religious scriptures, long practices and in the saying of wise persons. Common social values are co-operation, generosity, group harmony, faith, love, patience, careful listening and moderation in speech etc.

Social Benefits of Tourism Development

There exists one value or a set of values behind each and every task. Tourism development comprises mainly the monetary, aesthetic and socio-cultural values with the involvement of the local communities. For the continuous progress of tourism development, the role and importance of local community need to be assessed regularly. It is the local community that undergoes the changes due to tourism development. Tourism development brings two types of change in the life of its host. One is immediate change and second is the gradual change. The emerging of new building (restaurants, inns) to provide shelter to the tourists, better transport services, and increase in the opportunity of the employment comes under the category of immediate change. The gradual change involves the changes in the social and cultural values of that society that are not visible immediately. These changes take time to be visible but the foundation of these changes are laid with the first brick of immediate changes. Social values come under the second category so its repercussion is visible after so long when it has taken place.

Theoretical Underpinning

Tourism development impacts the social values both positively and negatively. In the words of Hawkins, tourism is a goose that not only lays a golden egg, but also fouls its own nest. Keeping this statement in the mind, the impact of tourism on social values can be categorized among two types. One is bright side of tourism development on social values and second is the dark side of tourism development on social values. First, the bright side has been discussed and then the dark side.

Money is the life veins of a happy society. Money improves the living standard of the community. Tourism expands community facilities by providing facilities of infrastructure, entertainments, education and sporting facilities. Even the remote area is also well connected to the city due to its importance as a tourist spot. With the growth of income, the lifestyle of the community is also improved. The extra earned money except from the traditional sources can be used further for the welfare of the downtrodden society. The numerous acts of Dharma can be performed with the help of money.

Preservation of Cultural Heritage

Any planning for the development of tourism industry searches that what is in them which distinguishes them from other in the form of idea, way of life, architecture and aesthetic sense. In other words, what is in them that can be used as a showcase that may attract the attention of others. When this sense is developed in them and showcase of that differentiation attracts a lot of tourists around the world then the community becomes convinced and is affirmed to preserve the cultural heritage of idea, architecture and way of life due to the appreciation and recognition it has brought to them at the national and international level. The tourist spot becomes a symbol of the residents of that community. Tourism always promotes this type of awareness among the community member for the conservation of cultural heritage that would have been negligible if the tourism sector did not come forward. The community starts taking pride in the preservation and exhibition of their cultural heritage.

Promotion of Humanitarian Value

Every tourist is welcomed by the tourism industry and the community irrespective of his class, colour and creed. It means that tourism is now available to all categories of people who, without the help and solidarity of society, could never benefit from its advantages. It also implies all the beneficial fallout in the shape of greater well-being, stability, and self-fulfilment that a society can expect to derive from such an immensely broader range of people who participate in such activities. The local community also feels obliged to co-operate and become eager to know about the community of tourists and their way of living. Tourism exposes the community to the new vistas of social experiences. It provides first hand information to the local people who have never dreamt of going abroad. This brushes the narrow thinking in them and they start developing the sense of brotherhood for all.

Increases the Degree of Tolerance

With the development of tourism, the common man has been able to get rid of himself from the jealous and contemptuous attitude for other races. When one comes in contact of others it helps people to wash the wounds of history and they can walk together in a more free and friendly environment. The local community by looking at so many differences between the two types of society may undermine their own differences within their own society. If the local community can bear the presence of a stranger whose lifestyle is totally different from their way of living then it becomes easier for them to tolerate the slightest differences of social values in their own community.

Expansion of Outlook

Tourism provides the direct experiences of many cultures for the common man at a single place as it is not easy for everyone to visit many countries but the tourist spot becomes an epitome of the whole world. The community while coming into contact with the other world sometimes feel the need to look inside what is wrong in their values that keep them behind or underdeveloped from other parts of the world. This question puts them into the process of analyzing the values and beliefs of their society and they can weigh the values of different societies and their own society to accept the goodness and leave the badness. The attitude of one society to life may be idealistic or pragmatist; one society may promote individualism and second may prefer public welfare.

When they come in contact with one another they may well analyze the benefits and harms of their attitude of living a life. Exchange of thoughts with the tourists helps them in realization that the need and cause of sorrow for whole humanity is the same. They ride on the same boat. And these feelings develop a sense of humanism not only for their own community but for the whole world. The member of the community starts giving one another comforts and let the tourists allow to use their personal belongings as well in case of long stay of tourists. The whole world for them becomes a house and they feel alike when their outlook expands.

Displacement of Residents from the Tourism Site

The local people are removed from the place where they have been living for ages. A sense of alienation is developed amongst them and it is not an easy task to leave the paternal place. Both those who leave the paternal place and second with whom they start living in another place undergo severe mental pressure and a sense of insecurity coupled with lack of faith which keeps their mind alarming day and night. They feel afraid of one other due to the fact of strangeness. A community depends on the local sources for the availability of daily routine things. Sometimes their rights to use the natural environmental resources are also banned for the commercial purpose only.

Promotion of Bad Habits

A person goes on a tour with travel motives and travel activities. One of the major travel motives is mental relaxation. A man takes a tour when he feels relaxed and free of worries and intends to enhance them. No one takes a tour when his heart is filled with sorrows and tensions. The most common activities involve visiting museums, experiencing nature, and trying local food. For these activities, he starts saving money to spend on the tour. He controls himself for months so that he can take a free life and can live his life the way he wants to live. Human beings can become nosier, more vulgar and more obnoxious in their approach to spend holidays. Therefore, one takes the opportunity of tour as a license to do what he wishes to do. He wants to untie himself from the boring life of daily routine and wants to do all activities which are not possible staying in the same place of his residence. This tendency of tourists promotes excessive drinking and gambling also. It sometimes even leads to the other social menaces such as drugs smuggling, prostitution and crime.

Changes in Lifestyle

Change only for the sake of change is not a change at all but a foolish imitation. The dressing styles, food habits, way of wishing goodness all are the result of adherence to the social values of a community. The tourists come with a lot of pompous attitude that brings the conflicts in the smooth social functioning of the society. They may also be pessimistic in their attitude to life and may undergo a negative psychological change. They may switch over to those unwanted changes in the lifestyle which neither suit their social values nor the geographical situation of their locality. Moreover, the long stay of any visitor in a single place may influence the local issues and concerns of the community.

Serenity of the Social Values is Hampered

Many communities do not like the entry of the outsiders. The composite nature of the community that involves the common belief system and manifestation of those through the festivity cannot be shaken only for the sake of monetary purpose. Traditional ceremony of any society may be lost in other activities if it is performed for monetary purpose rather than the real performance of traditional values. The smooth functioning of the social values is disturbed due to the entry of outsiders. The serene place of societal life is ravaged by the speculators. The life of the family is disturbed and the local people may fed up with the regular arrival of the outsiders and they may think in vice-versa of the saying *Atithi Devo Bhav* to *Atithi Tum Kab Jaoge*. The involvement of the people other than the community takes the loftiness of the celebration of festivals and festivity. Many people resist the involvement of outsiders in their affairs and some prefer the involvement of the tourists compulsory to attend the ceremony. This leads to conflicts among the local people of that community.

A shared understanding of the role of tourism and cultural values is critical. We must understand and treat equally all the aspects of tourism rather than focusing upon it for monetary purpose only.

Social Consciousness

Different social values are created in different societies. The nature of social values is such that even in the same society the same social value is manifested in different ways although the values are the same. But at the broader level, the general form of social values of the society should be known to the both: the host and the guest. Both the host and the guest should have a basic knowledge about the dressing style, eating habits and way of life so that minimum conflict arises between the hosts and guests. Some sort of common feeling must be developed before interaction of both the societies.

Undoubtedly, both hosts and guests are influenced by their separate cultural and social values but more responsibilities lie on the shoulder of guests as far as the question of way of living is concerned as the saying is "when in Rome, do as the Romans do". In turn, more responsibilities lie on the shoulders of hosts in relation to the safety measures, facilities, convenient staying and in creation of environment that reduces the sense of strangeness as soon as possible. When trust is built up then sharing of social values is possible.

Sense of Oneness

Undoubtedly, the society is run by social values even though the virtue has the same importance for all the people. The basic value behind every value is only one that can help in realizing the sense of oneness i.e. *Atamvat pashyati*, meaning to treat other people in the same manner as you want be treated by them. No one likes to be cheated by others, no one likes to be abused by others and no one likes others meddling with their personal matters. If one expects this kind of behaviour from others, he/she in turn should also respect the other individuals in the same manner. Hence, both the host and the guest should be aware of this value.

Conclusion

Tourism generally promotes a broader outlook by knowing the world around; the local community can be capable enough to minimize their own local differences among themselves. But at the same time, they may become over protective to preserve the differences that untie them from the whole world. Both the positive and negative side of tourism development can be analyzed from different perspectives and further the bright side of tourism development must be strengthened and the dark side of it should be minimized as far as possible.

References

Altinay, L., Sigala, M. and Waligo, V. (2016), "Social Value Creation through Tourism Enterprise" *Tourism Management,* 54, pp. 404-417.

Haulot, A. (1985), "The Environment and the Social Value of Tourism", *International Journal of Environmental Studies,* 25(4), pp. 219-223.

Mehmet, M., Hines, K., Graumann, C. and Greibrokk, J. (2010), "Relationship between Personal Values and Tourism Behaviour: A Segmentation Approach", *Journal of Vacation Marketing,* 16(1), pp. 17-27.

Index